PERFECT
Strangers

redefining intermarriage

Rabbi Avraham Jacobovitz

Published By ELIYAHOO College Outreach Network

A project of JAAM
Jewish Awareness AMerica

15221 West Ten Mile Rd.
Oak Park, MI 48237
www.eliyahoonetwork.com

Distributed by FELDHEIM PUBLISHERS
PO Box 35002/ Jerusalem, Israel

208 Airport Executive Park
Nanuet, NY 10954
www.feldheim.com

Perfect Strangers

Acknowledgements

One of the central themes of the Torah is appreciation - to have a continuous awareness of the goodness G-d bestows upon us every single moment. This concept far surpasses the ordinary realm of obligation. It is rather the most basic characteristic of humanity.

First and foremost, my deepest thanks are obviously to the Almighty for everything in my life and specifically for the privilege of being able to write this book.

Secondly, to my dear wife, Bayla, my partner in life, for always being there for me, constantly encouraging me to continue my work in spite of all the difficulties and challenges.

To my dear parents, my father, Rabbi Jeoudah Jacobovitz, of blessed memory, and my dear mother Rebbetzin Sheine D. Jacobovitz, may she live for many years in good health and happiness for everything they have done for me.

To my dear in-laws, Rabbi and Mrs. Moshe Bunim Pirutinsky, for treating me like one of their own children.

To my wonderful children (both my own and those who have joined our family by marriage) and all my sweet grandchildren.

Numerous people have contributed to the successful publication of this book, some directly and some indirectly. My sincere thanks to all of them. I would like to mention specifically the following individuals and families who have directly enabled this project to become a reality:

Mrs. Alice Berlin

Mr. and Mrs. Max Berlin

Dr. and Dr. Barry Braver

Mr. and Mrs. David Feber

Mr. and Mrs. Avraham Goodfriend

Mr. and Mrs. Howard Greenstein

Mr. and Mrs. Seymour Greenstein

Mr. and Mrs. Robert Koltai

PERFECT STRANGERS

Dr. and Dr. T. Barry Levine
Mr. and Mrs. Boruch Yisroel Levine
Mr. and Mrs. Howard Loebmann
Mrs. Sandra Loebmann
Rabbi and Mrs. Dov Loketch
Dr. and Mrs. Aharon Meer
Rabbi and Mrs. Yitzchak Mashitz
Rabbi and Mrs. Joseph Nusbaum
Mr. and Mrs. Yaakov Potesky
Mr. and Mrs. Neil Schloss
Mrs. Lois Shiffman
Mrs. Leo Storch
Dr. and Mrs. Robert Tawil
Mr. and Mrs. Brent Triest
Mr. and Mrs. Glenn Triest

Special thanks to Rabbi Yisrael Isser Zvi Herczeg of Jerusalem, Israel, for his translating and editing assistance, Mrs. Charlotte Friedland of Monsey, New York for her most skillful editing work, Mr. Stuart J. Snider, Mrs. Yocheved Freedman, Mrs. Miriam Maor, Mrs. Susan Tawil for their invaluable insights.

To Ms. Sheli Tinkelman for her instrumental involvement and support of this publication. To Ms. Devora Perlstein, for her artful design and layout.

Avraham Jacobovitz

Introduction

Making An Informed Decision

You or someone you know may be considering an interfaith marriage. If so, you have likely learned that intermarriage is a painful and delicate topic among many Jews. This is because marriage between a Jew and a non-Jew has for centuries been considered out of the question by most Jews. This attitude has eased in our generation. Today, intermarriage is common; the vast majority of our people see no reason to limit their marriage prospects only to Jews.

There are numerous reasons for this phenomenon. Primarily, it is because most Jews today have only a faint notion of Jewish history and religion, and what they do know is often distorted or incomplete. Sometimes I ask groups of Jewish students, "Who was the mother of Jesus?" They quickly respond, gladly and in unison, with the correct answer. To the question, however, of "Who was the mother of Moses?" there is silence.

How can a Jewish man or woman contemplating marriage make an informed decision on intermarriage when most Jews don't know what it means to be a Jew? How can we discuss the deep concept of Jewish marriage when the sanctity of marriage itself has been trivialized and often utterly debased by the society around us?

In addition, many people who are children of one-parent families say openly that because of what they have seen in their own or others' homes, they have no intention altogether ever to marry. Now, if they have little knowledge of Judaism, and marriage is considered at best a social ritual - and, at worst, a farce - the notion of excluding non-Jews as mates is meaningless, absurd and racist.

Perfect Strangers is an effort to explore the basics and discuss the big picture of intermarriage. The issue will be framed in the context of vibrant Jewish living in today's world, not simply as a carryover from bygone generations.

Before we can discuss the Jewish concept of marriage, we must first understand the human experience from a Jewish standpoint. We need to find out:

- What is the purpose of life?
- What are the essentials of human relationships in general, and, specifically, the relationship between men and women?
- What is love?
- What principles of Judaism are relevant to marriage?

After addressing these points, we can pursue the following issues:

- The philosophical aspects of intermarriage and why they matter
- Why interfaith marriage is not an issue of bias and bigotry
- Practical, real problems that face every intermarried couple

I ask that the reader not arrive at any personal conclusions until after examining this book in its entirety. A partial reading is liable to leave a distorted picture. I hope that this volume will be a lucid aid to those who sincerely want to understand the real issues with intermarriage from both an intellectual and deep-rooted Jewish perspective. *Perfect Strangers* will help you better understand the challenges of intermarriage and ways to deal with its ripple effects.

Contents

Why Are We Here?

CHAPTER 1

Why Are We Here?

During a lecture I gave to a group of social workers, I asked, "Let's say that you're treating an ailing eighty-five-year-old, someone who has lost most of her eyesight and suffers from depression. You want to give this person encouragement and vitality. What would you say?"

I was taken aback by the thoughtlessness of the responses. One social worker said, "I'd say, 'See what a nice day it is outside? It's beautiful!'" I reminded her that the patient is blind and cannot see the beautiful day. And what if outside it's cold and rainy?

Another said, "Think about your children. They are so wonderful!" I asked her, "What if she has no children, or what if they are not so wonderful? What then?"

1

"I don't know...that would be a problem," she answered, hastily adding, "But they usually have nice children or grandchildren."

I said to the group, "Then if this elderly person would ask you what is the point of life, you would answer that it's the children. And then the point of the children's lives would be their own children. Please tell me, what would the ultimate objective be?"

So what *is* the point of life? One of the greatest of Jewish thinkers, Rabbi Moshe Chaim Luzatto, wrote in his classic Hebrew work, *Mesilat Yesharim* (*The Path of the Just*), in discussing the subject of life after life, that it is illogical to believe that human life on earth is the objective of this world. If we look at the time that mankind has lived on this Earth, we would see that much of it has been spent suffering. Even people who seemingly lead a "good" life expend most of it on hard work, painful experiences or bothersome tasks. In the context of a total lifetime, the time spent experiencing true pleasure is very brief.

The purpose of mankind has been debated by thinkers and philosophers, Jewish and non-Jewish, in virtually every culture and generation. If we stop to think about it, we realize that the point that they all have in common is that their search is predicated on the idea that Man *has* a purpose. The notion that all of mankind is just an accident of nature, with no goal and having no meaning, is relatively recent. It is what gives so many people today the aimless, vague sense that their lives must be based on short term satisfactions. It then follows that morality must be relative in every instance: what seems okay for the moment will do.

Judaism rejects the idea that human beings evolved to fill some ecological need and have no more purpose than a jellyfish or a weed. Judaism restores our dignity by affirming that Man is different from everything else in the world because he has something unique: a soul.

What is a soul? It is a spiritual core that originated in a dimension not seen or felt in this physical world. Judaism ascribes to the concept of spiritual realms, regions currently undetectable by scientific means. The lofty nature of the soul stems from its source of truth: God, who is the ultimate giver. A person senses his soul when he feels compelled to give or be kind to others, particularly if his conduct exceeds the norm. Countless people have thus put their own lives in danger to save others, even a stranger. Your soul is that voice telling you that life is not meaningless, that you have true purpose. Your soul is eternal and pushes you to actions that will give you spiritual satisfaction in the long run.

The more deeply we reflect the more we realize that humanity itself is the wonder of wonders! Both in the physical and the spiritual realms, people search for a balance of these elements that are sometimes complementary and sometimes in conflict. Let's look at Man's essence another way.

Two people stand before us: One weighs 300 pounds, and the other weighs 100 pounds. Who is more of a human being? One might conclude that the 300 pound specimen is three times the human being as his 100-pound companion. Take another example: We have one person whose body is whole, and another who is missing an arm. Who is more of a human being? If we were to answer "the one with both arms," it would disturb, even anger, any rational individual.

No one should judge another's humanity based on weight or physical condition. But why not? Doesn't a man feel better when he is freshly showered, shaved, and wearing nice, clean clothes? Does not a woman feel more attractive when she is made up, wearing stylish clothes, and feels that her appearance reflects her personality? We highly prize these purely physical satisfactions and attributes. Why, then, does having substantial weight not enter into the picture? Why do we not regard more physical weight as providing more humanity? It is clear to everyone that one's body is not one's essence. A body is but an external facade. Yet if the body is not the real person, what is?

We must return to that special entity, the soul. Jewish sages have explained that the body is like an envelope, concealing the soul within. This hidden force is the energy that drives us. The marionettes at a puppet show give the impression that they are jumping and laughing on their own. But every child understands that someone else is pulling the strings.

It is noteworthy that the Talmud calls a human being a "small world," a microcosm. The Hebrew word for "world" is *olam,* related to the word for "hidden," *ne-elam.* We see only the world's - and a person's - exterior. Their infinite secrets are hidden from us.

Of course, although we don't understand it, this concealment is for our benefit. The Midrash (a talmudic commentary on the Torah) relates that there was once a child in ancient Jerusalem carrying a covered pot. A Greek visitor asked him, "What do you have in that pot?" The child replied, "If my mother wanted you to know, she wouldn't have covered it." Likewise, we sense that we have a soul; and we can delve somewhat into its purpose through study of Jewish texts. But deep down we know that we cannot fully fathom its essence. The spiritual dimension is so far beyond our experience that we call it "holy," which essentially describes something separated from this physical world.

Once we have identified our very essence, the core of our *self,* we are ready to discuss - *why are we here*? Torah scholars have summed up the answer to this quandary in two Aramaic words, "nahama d'kisufa", which freely translates as: "bread of shame". Sounds mystical, but it is really brilliantly simple.

In God's world of truth, there is a logical rule. No Godly being can truly enjoy anything unless it is deserved. Imagine if a high school dropout would be randomly awarded a doctorate in nuclear physics. Is this an honor? He knows the truth, that it is completely undeserved. He would in fact be insulted and shamed by such a gesture.

The human soul, which is part of God himself, certainly would never be able to enjoy the eternal goodness that God would have bestowed upon it undeservedly. It is for this reason, to avoid the so-called "bread of shame", that God created an arena of true freedom of choice in this world. God, in his infinite wisdom, constructed this world to be imperfect *by design.* In order to enable a Godly being to enjoy eternal bliss, God provides opportunities for him to *earn* reward through struggle and self refinement. In addition to the everlasting spiritual gains, God rewards humanity (Adam and Eve and their descendents) with some fringe benefits for their efforts while still in this life on earth. The ultimate pay, however, is given during the afterlife which our sages call *olam haba,* the future world. So the reason we are here, is to refine ourselves through life's challenges, thereby gaining eternal fulfillment. But what does all of this have to do with marriage?

As we proceed, it will become clear that with this background, we are better equipped to consider the spiritual reasons why men and women marry.

Chapter One ——————————————————

Man and Woman

CHAPTER 2

Man and Woman

The Torah is meant to enlighten us about the nature of this world and our role in it. Most people have a superficial understanding of "Bible stories," but our sages, the Talmudic scholars who have made its study a lifelong project, reveal the deeper messages within it.

If we examine the Biblical account of Creation, for example, we discover an interesting distinction. Humankind's order of creation differs from that of the animals. God created both male and female animals at the very start. But the first human was androgynous, with both male and female elements. According to the narrative, the Creator commands this first man, Adam, to name all the animals, i.e., intuitively to understand the essence and purpose of each of them and identify them according to their function in this world. Only after fulfilling this commandment does Adam realize that he himself has no mate. And only then God separates his male and female attributes, in the process creating woman as a separate entity.

What does all of this mean? If, ideally, the feminine and masculine form a single being, why did God separate them? And if it is best that they be distinct, why did the Creator form them as a single being in the first place, separating them only after Adam expressed his need? Why not create things as they should be from the start?

The Bible's message is that, in God, the masculine and the feminine coexist. Furthermore, as Man was created as a likeness of God (termed "in His image"), he at first reflected the all-inclusiveness of his Divine Creator in having both masculine and feminine components. But, as we will explain in detail below, for humans to derive the maximum benefit from their earthly existence and perfect themselves to the highest degree, it was necessary to separate woman from man.

This separation created the field of interaction between the two of them that allows them to merge their Divine aspects through a dynamic relationship based on mutual give and take. It allowed for the state of marriage in which perfect divinity is expressed. This is why the happiest and holiest occasion in Jewish life is the marriage celebration. It is through marriage that separate entities join to complete their Divine mission.

Man and woman, then, are equal in the quality of their Godly aspect. But equality does not rely on sameness. They are, as Jewish religious literature clearly explains, different in their attributes, their natures, their bodies, and their souls. These differences enhance their relationship and make it possible for both to achieve their full potential.

How Do We Reach Our Spiritual Potentials?

Let me begin with a simple story. One day, when I came home after my weekly shopping trip, my two-and-a-half year old son came out to greet me. When he saw my full shopping bags, he asked if he could help me carry them. I tried to explain that the bags were too heavy for him. He started to cry and insisted stubbornly that he was big enough to help.

So I took a bag of potato chips out of one of the bags and asked him to take it inside. His joy knew no bounds. He proudly ran into the house, clutching the bag of chips, and shouted, "Look Mommy! I'm helping Daddy!" Of course, my wife smiled and shared his jubilation. Later, she told me how happy I had made the little fellow.

In a sense, this is the way God treats us. He allows us to do something and gives us the good feeling that we are "helping" Him. But it is no sham; His purpose is to empower us to achieve the most important things in life.

The child's need to help, and the feeling of accomplishment and self-worth that results from helping, gives us a peek into the human soul's innermost recesses. As far as the Creator Himself is concerned, He has no "need" for Man's worship or "good" activities. The deep-rooted need to help and to treat others with kindness stems from Man's essential similarity to his Creator, the ultimate source of benevolence. The Creator developed an elaborate system to help Man to fulfill his objective. Jewish religious texts call it "Building a World on Kindness."

This system has two major components:
- Man's kindness toward his fellow man
- Man's "kindness" toward God

In the Ten Commandments, through which the principles of faith and morality were imparted to the Jewish people, five commandments pertain to the relationship between Man and God, and five pertain to interpersonal relationships. Briefly stated, they are:

1. I am Hashem (a name of God), your God, Who has taken you out of the land of Egypt, from the house of slavery.

Chapter Two ————————————————

2. You shall not recognize the gods of others in My presence. You shall not make yourself a carved image or any likeness of that which is in the heavens above or on the earth below or in the water beneath the earth. You shall not prostrate yourself to them or worship them...

3. You shall not take the Name of Hashem, your God, in vain...

4. Remember the Sabbath Day to sanctify it...

5. Honor your father and your mother...

6. You shall not murder.

7. You shall not commit adultery.

8. You shall not steal.

9. You shall not bear false witness against your fellow.

10. You shall not covet your fellow's house...wife...or anything that belongs to him.

If the purpose of these rules is to civilize individuals and bring order to society, it is perplexing that the commandments that apply to the relationship between Man and God appear before those that apply to inter-human relationships. Conventional wisdom has it that the true quality of a Man is measured by how he functions within society. His relationship with God falls into the private realm of "religiosity," and has no bearing upon whether we view a person as good or bad.

Chapter Two

But the Ten Commandments teach us that this "conventional wisdom" is a mistake. Allow me to explain.

Sometimes, when I speak about Judaism, I pose the following question to my audience: Take a person who is "ultra-Orthodox," someone who is very meticulous about his religious observance. He eats only food that is strictly kosher. He prays with devotion three times a day. He buys the most carefully made and expensive matzah for Passover. But he is utterly insensitive to the feeling of other people. He is dishonest, arrogant, and a vile gossip. Do you consider this person righteous or not?

Almost everyone answers that such a person is depraved. And they are 100% correct. Judaism says unequivocally that someone who mistreats others is evil.

But what about the opposite situation? Take a person who is devoted to the needs of others. He tries to cheer the broken-hearted and the poor. But although he has studied philosophy and is convinced of the existence of a Creator, he chooses to ignore Him. Perhaps he has chosen to join a pagan cult, violating the very first of the Ten Commandments. Is this person righteous or not?

In this case, most people answer that this person is righteous, and that his religious practices are his own business.

Chapter Two ————————————————————

I then respond with the following story: A man is walking down the street one sunny day and encounters a homeless person. For whatever reason, they strike up a conversation. He discovers, much to his surprise, that he actually likes this tattered vagabond. The next day, they meet again and converse. This happens day after day, until the two become close friends. A short while later, the poor man is diagnosed with a deadly disease that requires long and expensive treatment. His odds of survival are slim. His new friend devotes himself completely to caring for him, eventually quitting his job so that he can spend all of his time helping the sick man. Can anyone possibly deny the nobility and selflessness of this man? He deserves a Nobel Prize!

But then we find out one detail about him that we did not know before. Our noble and selfless friend has a mother who devotedly and lovingly raised him. She, too, has been critically ill with this same deadly disease for three years now. For three years she has not had a moment free of suffering. But her noble and selfless son has not so much as called her on the phone all that time. She is in the same hospital as his homeless friend, but he hasn't even looked in on her once. He is angry with her. You see, three years earlier he called her up one night, and she said that she couldn't speak with him because she was busy. She asked if he wouldn't mind calling back in half an hour. He was personally offended and hasn't spoken with her since. Do you still think this man is so noble?

Chapter Two

We have two options here: We could say that he is emotionally disturbed and forgive him for treating his mother so disgracefully. Or we could say that he is a mean-spirited ingrate who only treated the homeless person kindly to satisfy some personal psychological need. Either way, he is no saint.

So, then, the sequence of the Ten Commandments teaches us that a person who is considerate of his fellow Man, but callously ignores his Creator, is missing the point. God gave him the gift of life, yet it's been years (probably since his bar mitzvah) since he has so much as called. He wants to be a noble spirit, but doesn't realize that he must first have a relationship with God before he can be truly altruistic in regard to his fellow Man. "A world built on kindness" must have its foundation on recognizing God's kindnesses to us. We build on that foundation in all of our successful human interactions.

With this introduction, let us proceed to the topic of interpersonal relationships.

Chapter Two ————————————————

The Ground Rules
of Interpersonal
Relationships

CHAPTER 3

The Ground Rules of Interpersonal Relationships

It is rare to find a family in which everybody-including aunts, uncles, and cousins - gets along with each other. The rate of divorce is increasing at a dizzying pace. Many people have concluded that it's not worth it to get married in the first place. Why have we come to this state? What's going on here?

Of course, this is a complicated situation for which there are no simple answers. Nevertheless, it seems to me that the problem of proper communication between people lies at the core of the matter. Let's examine how these difficulties develop.

Everyone's life is composed of a system of relationships. From an early age, people develop all sorts of connections with their environment. An infant in her crib connects with her blanket and toys. Just try to take them from her! She'll cry as if she is being physically attacked.

Soon, relationships develop with parents, siblings, neighbors, with the storekeeper down the block, with teachers, with the school bus driver. All of these come under the category of "relationships," but each has a dynamic of its own. For example, if a child were to relate to his uncle exactly as he relates to his father, or to his cousin exactly as he relates to his grandfather, we would seriously worry about his mental stability.

In today's adult world, there are unfortunately many who suffer from an inability to discriminate between various types of interpersonal relationships. We have become accustomed to a sort of societal communism. This is expressed in many areas: in the way young people speak to their elders; in the way employers and employees speak with each other; and the nearly complete equality between student and teacher that sometimes borders on the jovial camaraderie of the student and the person who is supposed to be his guide in life.

This across-the-board amity purports to express the blessing of unity. It arose as the antidote to the serious problem of inequality that has indeed plagued Mankind; but exaggeration in the opposite direction is itself a severe problem. In truth, this social leveling eats away at the healthy system of relationships between people in different positions and leads to misunderstanding. It can lead to a blurring of the individual's sense of his own identity and is a strong factor in the confusion that reigns in the area of relationships between family members and between friends. The direct result is often a vast array of communication difficulties between spouses, friends, and family members.

How does this principle of blurred relationships and inappropriate communications operate in real life? Here's one example:

A couple turns to a marriage counselor for help. "It's been two years now since he's said that he loves me," opens the wife in her attack against her once-beloved husband.

The psychologist is shocked. Can this be? He turns to the husband and asks, "Has it really been that long?"

Now the husband gets angry. "This is ridiculous! It's been just two years since we took our marriage vows and repeated to each other, 'I love you, I love you, I love you.' I gave her my promise! Why is she accusing me of not loving her? Where is her trust in me? Is this all that my word means to her?"

_____ Chapter Three

This may sound funny, but the sad truth is that this husband is relating to his wife as if she were a business partner. He gave his word; he'll come through. He doesn't have to say "I love you" again any more than he has to call up his partner every day and say, "We're in business together."

Where is his mistake? It is in just one small point: A wife is not a business associate. It's a different relationship altogether, and the ground rules are not the same. But he had no idea that these relationships differ and that his communication (or lack of it) with his wife left her deeply disappointed. If he can learn how to relate to a spouse, the marriage can be saved.

So we see that achieving successful interpersonal relationships is a delicate, many-layered complex system of communications between individuals. These relationships are essentially built on three aspects of humanity:

(1) The physical - Intimacy, family closeness, living as neighbors, working together, and the like.

(2) The emotional - For valid reasons (including admiration), we feel kinship to one another. We root for a sports team because they represent the city in which we live, and we connect with them.

(3) The spiritual - We find commonality between our souls and between our spiritual aspirations. We have common beliefs that are expressed by a common lifestyle.

Chapter Three ————————————

Because we all are composed of these three elements, our system of relationships is based on connections with others involving these three areas. Sometimes the connection is limited to one person's emotional component. Sometimes it is limited to the spiritual component. Sometimes it involves a combination of the two, *e.g.*, the spiritual and the physical.

Of course, the strongest connections are the ones we call love and hatred. The positive connection between one person and another that causes happiness and a pleasant feeling is love. The force that divides people, causing ill feeling and animosity, is hatred.

Critical to any marriage is how we develop love and express it. Ever since human relationships began, volumes have been written on the definition of love. It all seems so simple, yet is somehow quite complex! What is the Jewish take on love?

What is Love?

CHAPTER 4

What is Love?

When I went to a new dry cleaner for the first time and picked up my cleaned and pressed clothes, I left with more than just fresh clothes. I left with a wonderful feeling, a real surprise. The plastic bag covering my suit had written on it the message, "We love our customers." What a warm feeling that gave me. Fantastic! They love me!

Wherever I go lately, I'm surrounded by endless love. Every store and every office loves me. Even the cab driver in front of me at the traffic light this morning loves me. After all, his bumper sticker says, "I love you!"

Does this "loving" society really know what love is? Is it a society that knows how to love? Is this not the same society that has a nearly 60% divorce rate?

It strikes me that when we attend a wedding and wish the newlyweds "mazal tov" (congratulations, good luck), what we are really saying is, "Mazal tov - maybe you'll be in the lucky 45%." Why bother with the fancy weddings and with all the pressure that they put on the bride and groom and their parents? So that only 40% of these marriages should succeed? And even out of those, how many are really successful? Many of the people involved in them would get out if they could. It is evident that many couples think that they are in love, but true love is, for them, really an unattainable ideal.

And how many marriages reach fulfillment in spiritual terms? Unfortunately, only a tiny minority of married couples benefit from marriage's spiritual treasures.

I remember the first time that I saw a bumper sticker that said, "Have you hugged your child today?" I found it very disturbing. "Is this what we have come to?" I asked myself. I have never seen a bumper sticker that says, "Have you eaten today?" or "Did you breathe today?" The instincts that accompany natural parental love should be strong enough to motivate parents to hug their children and tell those children that they are loved, without being reminded. Children have a deep need for love, and we have a deep need to express it.

That absurd bumper sticker shows us how far we have descended. We have stopped communicating in the ways we need most. Despite the recent tremendous advances in communications - cell phones, text messaging, email, to name just a few- many people feel terrible isolation today. It would seem that it should be impossible for people to feel lonely. Everyone has the tools to be in touch with friends and relatives whenever they want. But studies show, as do my counseling experiences, that a high percentage of the population suffers from severe and painful alienation.

In our society, most parents leave their children to be raised by babysitters. Even when the parents come home from work, they have but a limited relationship with their children. They are more interested in what some newscaster has to say than in the day-to-day problems with which their children struggle. The "family meal" is facing extinction, if it is not already gone. People hardly even find the time to speak with their spouses unless they have to. So what kind of love are people talking about? How has love disappeared?

The first step toward the answer is getting to the bottom of the problem: We must consider, what is the essence of love?

————————————————— Chapter Four

True Love

When I lecture on this subject, I often ask the audience the following: "Is there anybody here who is willing to come out and admit that he loves ice cream?"

Of course, I never have difficulty finding a volunteer willing to declare, "Of course, rabbi, I love ice cream."

The next question is, "Are you really sure that you love ice cream?"

"Sure," the volunteer answers. "I'm not lying to you. *I really love ice cream!*"

"Fine," I answer. "And please don't take my next question as an insult. But how do you treat your ice cream? Have you ever done anything for it? All that you want to do is to use it for your personal pleasure! What you really mean to say is that you *love to destroy* the ice cream."

The audience is usually quiet for a few moments before they burst out laughing. They see the absurdity of what I'm saying. This fellow has just said that he loves ice cream, but, instead of giving it a hug, he begins to devour it, enjoying it until there is nothing left. What nerve he has to call this love!

Chapter Four ————————————————

Now let's talk about you. Do you really love ice cream, or do you love to devour it? The sole basis for this "love" is the enjoyment of the sensations that it gives your palate and your throat.

How do you love the person whom you consider your true love? Upon sincere reflection, intellectually honest people will usually admit that in the majority of man-woman relationships, "ice cream love" dominates. Though it is tough to concede, they often come to the conclusion that the primary focus of their "love" boils down to self-gratification; what is most important is what the person will get out of the relationship with the other party.

No wonder those relationships break down entirely. So again we must ask, what is true love?

There is a widespread notion that Man's deepest need is to be loved. But our Jewish sages have provided a simple proverb that teaches us the deepest needs of the human soul: "More than the calf wants to nurse, the cow wants to do the nursing."

Judaism teaches that because we are created in the image of our Creator, our spiritual side wishes to emulate Him by being a *giver.* We need to give love even more than we need to receive it. The more people are conscious of their spiritual identity, the more in tune with this quality they will be.

To clarify this concept of love, let us delve into this spiritual need a bit further. A person who spends his life trying to obtain something for nothing is, spiritually, an unhealthy person. There is a statement in the Biblical book of Proverbs that is at first puzzling: "He who hates gifts shall live" (15:27). This requires further explanation. Will somebody who enjoys receiving a gift actually die because of it? Don't we see that this never happens? What is actually meant is that if a person loves receiving gifts, *i.e.*, he is always a taker rather than a giver, he is not really living. He simply does not understand the purpose for which he was created and is oblivious to the Divine dimension of his being.

Even if unaware that the need to give is a spiritual need, many people instinctively opt to be givers. We see that a childless couple will sometimes spend a fortune on all sorts of fertility treatments. Then they may give virtually all of their earthly possessions to adopt a child. Why? Do they really long for sleepless nights, dirty diapers, visits to pediatricians, and all the other pleasant things that accompany parenthood? Are they out of their minds? Why would they not prefer to spend their lives in a state of ease and romantic bliss, without the constant disturbance of those egocentric, high maintenance little beings that we call children?

The answer hinges on the essence of the soul's aspiration to contribute to others, and the feeling of satisfaction that the act of giving provides. The couple innately realizes that through their child they can *give* to a level not otherwise possible, to a degree that renders the continuing, expensive, and time-consuming inconveniences of parenthood inconsequential.

A person can certainly derive temporary and superficial pleasure from taking advantage of the material world's resources. He can even convince himself that he is happy and content. But eventually a person who is uninvolved in the advancement of society and does not contribute to its betterment feels an essential void in the depths of his soul. As he grows older, somewhere, deep within him, he begins to understand the depth of the illusion under which he has led his life.

What happens then? It depends on if he is still in a state in which he can change direction and has the strength to redirect his life's path. If so, there is still time to attain spiritual satisfaction. I have seen through my counseling that, unfortunately, when such an individual is already homebound by poor health, he finishes his life with a feeling of terrible emptiness and depression.

When people truly love with a "love" that is worthy of this sublime title, they feel tremendous pleasure in providing for the needs of their beloved. Consider, for example, a person who has a splitting headache on the afternoon of Yom Kippur, when the fast is at its hardest point. His four-year-old daughter comes over and says, "Daddy, I'm hungry!" The father leaves the synagogue to go home, which is a considerable walk. Once home, he makes his daughter a tasty sandwich with fresh bread, salami, mustard, and a pickle. He serves it on a plate. He pours a glass of juice for her. The father feels genuine pleasure and contentment from seeing his little girl sitting there, innocently munching on that sandwich. Every bite gives him more satisfaction, even though he himself is hungry and tired.

This is what I call "landing at the gates of love," meaning that this is within the parameters of "real" love, though it is not the ultimate illustration of "love." For despite that the father is mature enough to have overcome his selfish impulse to ignore her, and he derives genuine satisfaction from giving to his daughter, there is still room to argue that if it were his neighbor's child who had asked him to take her home for food on Yom Kippur, he would not have gone so far out of his way for her. He might not have enjoyed the whole idea. Our example, then, is not a perfect example of love, because a person's child is an extension of himself. Still, it does help to illustrate the concept of how deriving pleasure from the pleasure of others indicates genuine love.

If we deeply examine the topic of love, we arrive at a very interesting point. When a person gives to others, he indirectly gives to himself. Our sages have taught us this principle in an adage about charity: "More than the donor does for the poor man, the poor man does for the donor." This means that although it is the poor man who receives assistance from a financial aspect, from the far more important, spiritual, aspect, the poor man is giving his benefactor a very precious gift - the opportunity to give. The giver receives the realization of his soul's objective, which is giving to others. In Judaism, giving this opportunity to the donor is the greater of the two gifts involved in an act of charity.

This all sounds very nice. But people are by nature egocentric. We must ask, practically speaking, how does a person reach that state in which he can derive pleasure from *giving to someone else*? Here the Torah reveals to us a wonderful secret through the pithy statement, "You shall love your friend as yourself." The sages have told us that these few words encapsulate the fundamental principle that is the basis of the entire Torah. But that raises a question: If the Torah is the Divine blueprint for human life and achievement, why would this maxim be considered its foundation?

We have explained the centrality of genuine love to Man's essence. But the words "love your friend as yourself" still sound strange. If the other person is not your friend, is there no obligation to love him? Is it not important to love all of mankind? And what does "as yourself" mean? Do I have to love the other person exactly as I love myself? What if I don't love myself - am I then exempt from loving others?

In truth, the profound words "love your friend as you love yourself" teach us to apply the concept of genuine love. With "your friend," the Torah reveals to us that the only way to attain authentic love is to feel friendship and mutuality with others. Without the feeling of friendship towards others - if we feel that they are foreign to us - genuine love is impossible. The main challenge posed to us by the verse "You shall love your friend as yourself" is the art of developing the feeling of friendship.

Only after a person feels that another person is his friend will it come as second nature to help him and to love him. The more we give to others, the more we broaden our identities to include all of mankind within the idea of "me." From this perspective, one who gives also takes.

This is the spiritual instinct behind the natural human urge to have children. By giving life to another, the giver gains doubly. He gives his life meaning, and at the same time achieves a broadening of his own identity by the enlargement of his family.

The upshot of what we are saying is that the way to attain love is by finding the way to connect ourselves with others. Of course, within this system there are various degrees of friendship, such as those existing between husband and wife, parent and child, teacher and student, and friend to friend.

But the Torah invokes us to love others as we love *ourselves*, exposing an additional deep dimension of the human soul: a person has a duty to love himself. Yes, just so. For a person who does not love himself is not emotionally healthy. Our sages have already taught us that if a person does not care about himself and about his life, it is impossible to rely upon him to protect the lives of others. If he lacks concern for himself, he certainly lacks it for others, despite all of his declarations to the contrary. The Creator, therefore, in His wisdom, commanded us to love our friend *as ourself*, no more and no less. This may sound simple, but whoever reflects on it deeply will see that this is a very high level to reach.

In summary, genuine love (in marriage, as in all human relationships), expressed in the Torah passage as "You shall your friend as you love yourself," depends upon three points:

- "You shall love" - **genuine love** - not a superficial one. Not the way that you "love [to destroy] ice cream."

- "Your friend" - **the realization that every person is actually an extension of yourself** - connected to you with bonds of brotherhood. This is the secret of the bond of friendship and respect.

——————————————————— Chapter Four

- "As you love yourself" - **self-love** - and equating the love for your friend with it.

It is worth pointing out that the Christian Bible translates this verse as, "You shall love your *neighbor* as yourself." This mistranslation from the original Hebrew is a linguistic error and misses the thrust of the verse. The point is that the bond of friendship should be based on *affinity* between people, not mere physical *proximity.*

There are, indeed, various non-Jewish sects that preach this verse, yet encourage self-abnegation to the point of self-hatred. They destroy the very foundation of emotional health, which requires love of the self before one can truly love another.

Having examined the essence of love according to Jewish teachings, we may now take a step further toward understanding intermarriage - by examining Judaism and the unique identity of the Jewish people.

Chapter Four ————————————————

Judaism 101

CHAPTER 5

Judaism 101
What They Never Told You

What Judaism is Not

Allow me to share an old joke with you. It's been around since the 19th century, when many Jews lived in dire poverty in czarist Russia and were subject to frequent proselytization.

A Jew was in deep financial trouble. He was walking along the streets of his town when he noticed a poster that said in the name of the local church that any Jew who would convert to Christianity would be paid the handsome sum of 10,000 rubles. Despite his misgivings, the temptation of having enough money to solve his problems appealed to him. He went to the local priest who was delighted at the rare opportunity to convert a Jew. But the priest set one condition. He was worried that the Jew might revert to Judaism after converting, so he had him swear that for the rest of his life he would not eat gefilte fish, a uniquely Jewish food staple. The Jew didn't hesitate for a moment and swore that he would never again touch the stuff.

After he converted, the Jew returned home with the money in his knapsack. The priest was overjoyed, but he suspected that the Jew might not keep his word. So he hid out on Friday night in a location from which he could peer into the Jew's window. To his great surprise, the priest saw a table set in the traditional manner for the Sabbath, complete with lit candles. This angered him, but still, it was not a violation of the oath.

Then the Jew entered the room dressed in his Sabbath finery and sat at the table. He recited the traditional Kiddush blessing, then washed his hands and recited the blessing over two loaves of challah. This certainly did not please the priest, but still, it was not a violation of the oath.

But what happened next was unbelievable *chutzpah*. The Jew's wife brought to the table a tray of … yes… it was gefilte fish! The Jew helped himself to a portion and was about to take a bite. The priest could

Chapter Five ——————————————

no longer restrain himself. He jumped out of his hiding place, opened the door of the house, and screamed at the Jew, "Liar! Cheat! Give me back the money! You swore that you would never eat gefilte fish again!"

The Jew replied calmly, "Pardon me. I don't understand what you're so upset about. Sit down and let me explain. You're making a mistake. My wife went to the market this morning and bought some fish. In the kitchen, before she cooked it, she sprinkled water on it three times. Each time she said, 'From now on you are not fish. You are not fish. You are not fish.' I converted and so did the fish!"

Sounds funny? Well, in real life this type of fake and superficial spirituality is truly tragic. For too many Jews, Judaism has been reduced to eating Jewish foods, performing empty rituals, contributing to Jewish organizations, attending Jewish plays and concerts, and occasionally going to temple. To our misfortune, this has been the case for several generations: unknowingly, our people have been robbed, while still children, of their right to know and understand their authentic cultural and religious roots. They even may have been taught - subtly or overtly - that historical Judaism has no relevance to modern life, that it is best relegated to museums.

Of course, we have been taught to respect our roots, just as Italians respect their roots and the French theirs. After all, we have Jewish music (the Klezmer stuff played at Bar - and Bat Mitzvahs for a little while), Jewish jokes (usually self-denigrating) and a holiday that's not Christmas. It may not be much of a culture, but it's ours. And we don't mind sharing it.

Culturally speaking, what's wrong if an Italian man marries a French woman? Nothing at all! Each will learn about the other's culture and the children will be enriched by two cultures rather than just one! And if Judaism is simply one culture among many, there is really no problem with intermarriage.

But Judaism is not merely a culture. Nor is it an "identity." Even in Israel, where Jewish *identity* is inescapably strong but *education* about Judaism is weak, a recent study asked, "If you had the choice of being born as a Jew in Israel or as a non-Jew somewhere else, what would you choose?" A high percentage of the respondents answered that they would prefer to be non-Jews. Mere identity was not enough to keep them Jewish.

Is Judaism based on religious rituals, then, or a political leaning? Not really. Judaism is not dependent on activities that take place in the temple or synagogue. Nor is it focused on love of or support for the State of Israel. It is certainly not expressed by peppering one's speech with some random Yiddish words or phrases like *latkes*, *chutzpah*, and *oy vey*. Wearing a necklace with a Star of

David or a *chai* pendant does not express Judaism, though it does identify the wearer as someone who should know what it represents. It does mean that the wearer doesn't mind being singled out as a Jew.

That's a beginning, but it's not an end. Very often, that Jewish star means we think of ourselves as "hyphenated" Jews. We are Jewish-Americans, just as there are Irish-Americans, or Italian-Americans. So we're back to a cultural identification and, even there, only half of it is Jewish. It means we are just like everybody else, only we happen to be Jewish.

But the strange truth is that we are unable to be like all other people. Historically, the more Jews tried to assimilate among others, or at least to reduce Judaism to a nationality like others, the more they failed and suffered ostracizing by others. Even when they succeeded in penetrating non-Jewish society, intermarried, and considered themselves no longer Jews but, rather, part of the larger family of mankind - events generally proved that their Jewish origin was firmly rooted in the minds of the people around them.

"America is different," you say. I wish I could agree. But the experience of Jews in every part of this country is that there is a deep-seated and very real undercurrent of anti-Semitism that still exists in every strata of American society. Granted, it is politely well hidden in most places,

Chapter Five

perhaps even subconscious in many individuals. This is not the first time we Jews were under the illusion that we have become totally absorbed in the culture around us.

The Jews of early 20th century Germany serve as the best example of this self-delusion. They were the most "enlightened" Jewish community in the world. Many of them thought of their country as the exemplar of progress and equality for Jews. They held important positions in all areas of society. It was hard to distinguish them from other Germans. Some Jews and Germans had intermarried, apparently without repercussion.

Then Hitler rose to power, eventually enacting "grandfather" laws that identified anyone with a Jewish grandparent as a Jew. In Nazi Germany, every Jew, even one who considered himself non-Jewish, was hunted down and disaster followed. Secular Jews who had lived indistinguishably for generations among non-Jews in total peace and security suddenly found themselves being identified as Jews and turned in to the Nazis by their own neighbors.

Their experience prompted a good deal of questioning in the decades that followed: Why is it that the Jew is always singled out? Other cultures have melted into the societies around them; why is the Jew forever a Jew?

Chapter Five ————————————

So Judaism is not simply a culture, not an identity; nor is it just a religion or a political stance. From the standpoint of Jewish belief, no one just happens to be Jewish. If someone is born a Jew, it is because he or she has been given a uniquely Jewish purpose in this world. Our job is to try to understand it.

Now we know what Judaism isn't.

What *is* Judaism?

The Talmud makes the following statement: "This world is like a wedding hall." Very catchy and succinct, but what does it mean?

Many people are involved in putting a wedding together: there are those outside, passing the hall, wondering what all the commotion inside is about. People in the surrounding neighborhood who do not participate in the celebration are annoyed by the noise and the lack of parking space. Some people, such as the florist, the caterer and the band, participate indirectly in the event to make a profit. Others enjoy the wedding directly. These are the invited guests, some of whom make a pretense of happiness ("I'd rather be home watching the ballgame") and others who genuinely rejoice with the bride and groom. Then there are the relatives. In general, the closer the guests are to the family, the happier they are and the more they feel part of the great occasion. But who is at the center of it all? Everybody understands that everything begins and ends with the bride and groom, for they are the cause of the celebration.

So why is the world like a wedding hall? The Talmud is telling us that there are levels of participation in the Divine plan for this world. There are people in this world who are so far "out of it" that they have no idea of the spiritual nature and purpose of their existence and the importance of its details. Like the passers-by on the street, they only overhear that something is going on. There are those who enjoy the "music" from the periphery and understand the concept of sanctity, but have no interest in experiencing it. Then, there are some who are like the angry neighbors, who not only do not appreciate the concept of a relationship between humans and the Divine, they are upset and disturbed by the idea. For them, the existence of a spiritual world implies conscience and moral responsibility; the notion that the world is directed by an all-powerful God Who holds them responsible for all that they do angers them.

On the other hand, there are those (comparable to the florist or caterer) who are well aware of what is occurring but feel no part of it unless they experience immediate gratification in the form of payment for their participation. They might, by chance, happen to enjoy the music, as well. In other words, there are those who sometimes have patience for musing about spirituality and morality because they think that they will benefit from them, and at the end of a hard day's work they can eat a bit and have a drink or two, and continue their life's routine. Next come those who are guests at the wedding, but observe it detachedly. They support the concept of morality as a necessary obligation, just as guests at the wedding write out a check for the bride and groom.

But one thing is clear beyond anything else - it's all about the bride and groom. A fool arriving at the wedding might think that everything began that very day. You have a bride, a groom, a caterer, and a band. The couple is under the wedding canopy. Some of the guests cry, while others smile. They sit down to a meal, dance, and maybe drink a bit too much. That's it. On the other hand, someone who better understands things realizes that the bride and groom have gone through a lot to arrive at this milestone. They went through infancy, childhood, and adolescence, until they met and eventually committed to spending their lives together. Most of all, he realizes that the wedding is but the beginning of a joy that will last a lifetime and that will have everlasting effects.

In the Talmudic parable, who are the bride and groom, and how did they arrive at this moment in their lives? The *Song of Songs* and many Biblical and Talmudic parables identify God as the groom and the Jewish people as the bride. Of course, a parable such as this has many layers, and this is not the place to examine them all. What concerns us here is that God created the universe, and mankind, with a purpose. All of the preparations that comprise human history point toward the momentous event at which the Bride and Groom unite in marriage. The preparations for this event began when the Creator designed the world and later entrusted the Jewish people to accept His teachings and pass them on to all of humanity.

When the bride - the Jewish people - came of age, she agreed to the Creator's marriage proposal. That moment was after the Jews' exodus from Egypt, as they gathered at Mount Sinai seven weeks later. At that point, the entire, united Jewish nation was there- including the souls of all Jews to be born in the future- and accepted the Torah as a binding "marriage" contract from God. All future generations of this nation are obligated by the Covenant of mutual and eternal love forged at that time.

An imperfect comparison- but a comparison nonetheless- would be the Constitution of the United States. The American nation understands that its Constitution is binding for as long as it exists, by virtue of the agreement made by the Founding Fathers over two centuries ago, despite that no contemporary Americans signed it. So it is with the Constitution of the Jewish people. The Covenant between God and the Jewish people is eternal.

Chapter Five ———————————————

Unlike the US Constitution, however, the Torah is not regarded as merely a body of laws designed to impose societal order. It is a precious gift, a treasure bestowed by a loving Groom on his Bride, and accepted by her with joy and tender affection. The tenets of Judaism expressed in the Torah cover the entire spectrum of spiritual concepts and human experience from the patently simple to the infinitely deep. By following the Torah's principles, we become valued participants in this "wedding" to whatever degree we choose to become involved.

The sages who spend their lifetimes elucidating the Torah and relating it to human affairs have deduced three "foundations" upon which the world stands: Torah, worship, and doing kindness. Each is an area of human activity applicable to each of us, no matter what our circumstances. In this formulation:

- "Torah" refers to intense study of the Torah's wisdom. The Torah is the "User's Guide" to the world; it explains what the Creator expects from His spouse, the Jewish nation.

- "Worship" refers to worship in the heart. Though our minds tend to wander, we must focus daily on creating a deep bond with our Creator. This is accomplished through our daily prayers, character improvement exercises, and reflections on our spiritual development.

- "Doing Kindness" means *doing* acts of kindness actively, not just thinking about them. Being alert to opportunities to do kindnesses for other people creates a mindset, and the result is the refinement of our personality traits.

What the sages are telling us is that if every person would examine the Torah and relate it to his or her own life, recognize that God is actively involved in the life of every individual and responds to prayer, and develop a lifestyle dedicated to caring sincerely about others, that individual will not only be personally fulfilled, but is actually enabling the world to fulfill its mission as a habitat of peace and spiritual grandeur.

The Ten Commandments and Beyond

From here, we move to the principles that are a synopsis of all of the Torah: the Ten Commandments that were given to us through Moses on Mount Sinai directly from God. (We may note in passing that close to a billion Christians believe unhesitatingly in the Revelation at Sinai, as well as over one billion two hundred million Moslems. It is only a few million Jews who question this fact...)

The Ten Commandments are the essence of the Torah. The Torah comprises the Written Law (written in the Torah scroll) and the Oral Law (which explains the

Written Law and applies it to questions that arise). Moses received both the Written and Oral Law from God, then passed them down to the next leader of the Jewish people, Joshua. He, in turn, taught them to the Elders, and then it was transmitted through the generations of Jewish history to the *Men of the Great Assembly, the Tannaim, the Amoraim, the Savoraim, the Gaonim, the Rishonim, the Acharonim,* down to the rabbinic scholars of our own generation.

The Oral Torah, whose source is in the Written Torah, has four levels of understanding. In Hebrew, these are:

> *peshat* - simple meaning
> *remez* - allusion
> *derash* - exegetical meaning
> *sode* - mystical secrets

For most of us, the first three are a lifetime's work. Their study involves intellectual honesty, questioning, probing, and ultimately coming to a deeper understanding of truth. The Oral Law is studied from many texts: There are the Mishnah, the Babylonian and Jerusalem Talmuds, the halachic and aggadic (non-legal) Midrashim, as well as various ethical, philosophical, moral, and mystical works. These volumes contain the answers to all of Man's existential problems as well as the ways and means of coping with life on a daily basis.

Chapter Five

There is no wisdom in the world that the Torah does not include. In it, God gave us His beloved bride, the explanations of all of the mysteries of life in this world, and a glimpse into the depths of a spiritual dimension. The more effort that one devotes to it, the more one will understand and enjoy the splendid wisdom of our Creator. How sad and ironic it is to see Jews searching for "wisdom" and "spirituality" in the foreign fields of Buddhism, Christianity, Islam and various cults, without ever having looked seriously into their own eternal Torah, the ultimate source of wisdom.

Now that we have a deeper understanding of some of the principles of Judaism, we can summarize these qualities that make it unique - and look at them in a new light. We saw that Jewish living is based on:

1. Torah.
    Judaism is unlike other religions because it is based on knowledge and understanding. Passing the test of intellectual challenge leads us to deep and strong faith. Therefore, the study and comprehension of the Torah's wisdom - not unquestioning faith - is the most important principle of Judaism.

2. Worship.
    Judaism is not satisfied with superficiality. It demands constant self-improvement. The goal is to become someone who lives on a higher plane of life.

Chapter Five ————————————————————

To help us toward this we were given the Torah and its *mitzvot* (commandments), which have been designed to perfect us. They include the commandments not to speak maliciously about others; not to be envious; to give charity; to be concerned about the needs of others; to be kind to animals, etc. When we realize that improving our behavior is part of a Divine plan to bring harmony to the world and inner peace to the individual, we feel gratitude to our Creator who cares about us and gave us these gifts. When we feel connected to God, we want to communicate with Him. This natural impulse finds expression through our prayers.

3. Doing kindness.

The Torah, unlike other religions' doctrines, mandates practical actions rather than mere belief or good thoughts. As our sages have observed, "Our hearts follow our deeds." This world is a world of action. Yet our actions are based on the Jewish idea that the material world is spiritual at its core. Just as we see a table as a piece of wood rather than as the countless atoms that compose it, most people look superficially at the material world, unaware of its spiritual components. In Judaism, the material world is there only to serve spiritual ends. We do not, therefore, belittle the material world and look for holiness and spirituality through asceticism. On the contrary, it is through proper use and enjoyment of the material world, for our own needs and the needs of others, that we elevate ourselves. It is through performing the right actions (even though it is very difficult at times) that we reach our souls' spiritual goals and become worthy of a spiritual life that continues beyond death.

Now what does all of this have to do with your choice of a marriage partner? I thought you'd never ask.

Chapter Five ————————————————————

What is the Jewish Concept of Marriage?

CHAPTER 6

What is the Jewish Concept of Marriage?

In exploring Mankind's spiritual origins and the roots of Jewish nationality, we came across a remarkable fact. Every national culture in the world originated in a particular location, which became its homeland, and it was shaped by the common experiences of the people living there. This is true of virtually every group, whether it is Irish, Chinese, Tibetan or Mexican. Except the Jews. Jewish nationality did not originate on its later homeland. It became identified in Egypt and galvanized into a nation in the Sinai Desert. Its common experience was receiving the Torah and committing to keeping its laws. Homeland came later, and Jewish culture evolved directly from its Torah lifestyle. This unique origin - based on a spiritual

59

goal - explains why Judaism is portable and universal, why Jews have a kinship no matter which host culture they live in. Torah law's immutability gives the nation stability as well as identical values from generation to generation.

One of these values is the importance placed on marriage, a specifically human institution. Have you ever seen two horses waiting in line for a marriage license? No one objects to animals cohabiting, yet it is humans who seek to create a bond that will endure.

By the law of the land, there is no legal problem for a man and woman to live together all their lives without marrying. So what is it that impels an "enlightened" couple to spend so much time, effort, money, and emotional energy on a wedding, for no apparently logical reason? Tradition?

Despite the liberal position that marriage is an outdated institution, weddings are still common in every segment of society. It seems that something deep inside the human being pushes him/her toward this incomprehensible ceremony. Based on the information in the preceding chapters, I think that we can assemble the puzzle that forms the picture of marriage.

First, we must consider the structure of Man's essence and the uniqueness of his identity. Man is essentially a spiritual entity, residing in a physical shell.

Chapter Six ————————————————

Unlike animals, he possesses a soul. As we noted in Chapter 2, man and woman were originally two facets of a single body that were subsequently separated. This imbues them, like magnets, with the tendency to want to reunite. Animals, on the other hand, were created as male and female from the start. For them, there is no joy that is comparable to the celebration of marriage, the permanent reunification of the two separated parts, as there is to mankind.

The Talmud teaches us that as long as the male and female components of the soul have not found their complements, they lack a sense of wholeness. When these loving partners in the Divine soul meet in this world, after the years of separation necessary to prepare them for their reunification, there is no joy that can compare to it. They are like siblings reunited after decades of being apart. Because marriage exemplifies this ultimate happiness, the Bible is replete with comparisons of the relationship between God and the Jewish people to the marriage of a loving groom and bride. Many people sense this "soul-mate" relationship when they meet the right person and they want to ensure that the soul will never be torn apart again. Sanctifying their union with marriage is the ultimate expression of this need.

This stage - in which the soul's masculine and feminine aspects unite anew - is on the one hand an experience of joy and pleasure; on the other hand, it is a most difficult challenge. Because the two components of the soul grew up separately, they developed distinct identities and patterns of living. They are comfortable in their habits. Then, suddenly, they face the task of joining two worlds, two natures, and two families. Unlike simply living together, a couple who commit to marriage plan to be together permanently. In effect, they are saying they are ready to take on this long-range challenge, to work out their differences over many years. This situation holds the greatest potential for refining the character, purifying the soul, and raising spiritually to the point that full unity can be attained. This is the greatest satisfaction that can be gained from married life. On the other hand, it also can bring out the most extreme egocentricity and malevolence. The classical Jewish ethicists have therefore called marriage "the laboratory for the refinement of character and the human soul." This is a truly apt label.

Statistics that show that in the United States close to 60% of marriages end in divorce do not at all present an accurate picture. As we discovered in Chapter 4, in most situations where a man loves a woman or a woman loves a man, their love is only slightly more sophisticated than "ice cream love." What they mean is that they love to receive pleasure from one another, and their marriage is based on that mutual experience. And when the ice cream is finished, and along comes some other ice cream in a different cone, that's the end of the story.

Chapter Six ————————————————

But it goes much deeper than that. On the surface, the situation we just described looks like a marriage that failed. But that is incorrect; for it is unworthy of being called a marriage at all. As we have learned, marriage is a bond between the two components of a larger soul, the male soul and the female soul. But, in most cases, the husband and wife are not conscious of this and fail to develop their spiritual identity. They receive physical, emotional, psychological or financial benefits from their marriage - but the marriage has not brought them the lasting happiness they thought that it would.

A Jewish marriage is based on two aspects (and indeed the traditional Jewish wedding ceremony expresses both): the reservation of this particular woman for this particular man, to the exclusion of anyone else; and the public declaration that this couple now forms a single unit. The Hebrew word for marriage, *nisuin,* comes from the word meaning "to lift up."

The word itself speaks volumes about the purpose of a Jewish marriage and what it should mean to the couple. If the marriage is founded on a spiritual base, *i.e.,* the unification of the soul's male and female components- and if the partners' goal in marriage is to rise spiritually through the mutual kindness that results from true love- then the marriage will "lift" the couple to a sublime plateau. This will not occur if the marriage's objective is the derivation of physical and emotional pleasure, that is, a mere mutual exchange of self-gratification in which each party is willing to give the other a bit of ice cream. In the end, each of them will enlarge the scope of egocentricity and begrudge the other's ice cream to the point where either the marriage will collapse, or the two partners will reconcile themselves to lives of loneliness.

Isn't it amazing how the Hebrew language expresses entire concepts in one word? That is because this holy language - the language of the Jewish people in which the Torah was written - is in itself one of the layers of wisdom within the Torah. Here's another fascinating insight on marriage, based on Hebrew language.

The Hebrew word for "man" is *ish*. The word for "woman" is *ishah*. The spellings of these words are almost identical. (In Hebrew characters they are *aleph, yud, shin* and *aleph, shin, hey*, respectively.) Each contains the letter *aleph,* a tertiary sound that can be spelled as *i* or *e, and* the letter *shin* - a *sh* sound. They differ only in that the word for man includes a *yud - y* - and the word for woman ends with the letter *hey - h.* These two letters - *y* and *h* - combine to spell one of the Names of God. There is profound meaning here. The sages point out that if the couple brings God into their marriage, lifting their union to a spiritual level, the marriage functions as it should, bringing them great, fulfilling joy. If they remove God from their relationship, the remaining letters, *aleph* and *shin,* spell the word *esh,* which means "fire." The "fire" of selfishness and raw passion eventually will take over, for materialism without spirituality is a blazing fire.

In *The River, the Kettle, and the Bird: A Torah Guide to a Successful Marriage* (Feldheim, 1987), Rabbi Aharon Feldman presents a valuable description of marriage. (I highly recommend careful study of this book.) In short, he says that marriage consists of three stages:

1. The initial stage is like a river that connects two cities; it serves as the channel by which goods are shipped from one to the other. Similarly, the couple opens good relations between themselves and delivers "goods" of various sorts to one another. Each fulfills the other's needs, but they remain two distinct entities. The connection between them can be compared to a business relationship.

2. The second stage of marriage can be compared to a kettle of water resting on a fire. The fire and the water both cooperate toward achieving the same end - to provide boiling water. The kettle that separates them allows them to coexist and to collaborate toward attaining the mutual goal. In the parallel stage of marriage, the couple works together toward a mutual goal, but each has a distinct task, which he or she pursues separately.

3. The third stage is compared to a bird, which has two means by which it can propel itself - its wings and its feet. Each has its own time and place to function, yet each constitutes a part of the same body. The wings and feet are always together as two parts of the same being. When a couple reaches this stage, they are perfectly united.

Such marriages are rare. There are couples who live out their lives together in peace, harmony, and tranquility, but they are still not genuinely married in the spiritual sense. For there are men and women who can indeed be very compatible when it comes to their emotional and physical needs. They are content with this bit of "ice cream" that they have. Perhaps they have brought some original twist to it. Because they are good-natured, they are nice to each other. However, the extent of their unity is limited to the physical and the emotional realms, not to the soul, and they have not reached the goal of marriage-the complete unification of the soul, and the deep joy this brings.

The Sanctity of a Jewish Marriage

As a guide to physical and spiritual fulfillment, the Torah addresses every aspect of human life. A basic concept of Judaism is that God created everything to benefit us, and we are meant to enjoy the world in all of its beauty. Unrestricted access, however, ultimately results in

Chapter Six ———————————————————————

chaos. So in His Torah, God informs us that restrictions are necessary, even in the area of human sexuality. Laws on marital relations, for example, include prohibitions of incest and same-sex unions. In light of our understanding of marriage being the reunification of a soul that has been split into its male and female components, these restrictions are perfectly logical.

How can a couple reach a spiritual level in their marriage? Judaism views the husband and the wife as members of a team with a common goal. If we have a bicycle built for two riders, one person can ride it by himself, but with difficulty, and he may never be able to get to his destination. If two people ride together, however, the bicycle will move along smoothly, and the riders will reach their destination quickly and efficiently. In other words, both members of the marriage team must have the same objective and must cooperate to reach it. This is just as true in the spiritual realm as it is in the physical.

All of this talk of spirituality in marriage may have you thinking that Judaism frowns upon physical pleasure. Not so. Unlike many religions' attitudes that regard the physical love between a husband and wife as something sinful or shameful, Judaism regards their love as noble and exalted. There are many statements in classical Jewish sources that underscore the importance of the physical and emotional merging of the couple. They speak of the imperative for both spouses to remain attractive to each other physically, and for the wife to be as precious to her husband as a newlywed bride. The monthly renewal of marital love via the laws of "family purity" is a vehicle for this freshness, built into Jewish marriage by the Torah. (There will be more on this below.) The common denominator is that they regard the physical as important, but not an end unto itself. A proper physical intimate relationship is a means of bringing the Divine Presence into the marriage.

So what's the catch? You may look at the last sentence and think that it's in the word "proper." No, that's not a catch. Judaism is not advocating a marital relationship that is prim or unsatisfying. A proper physical relationship in Judaism is one that does not demean either partner. Read that again. It's simple, but basic.

The human body, although it is physical, is a receptacle of the highest degree of holiness. This is what gives it its value and its destiny. To demean the body is to demean the soul. If one takes the God-given body provided for the lofty purpose of expressing love and begetting children, and misuses it solely to fulfill sensual desires, one is denying the uniquely human (and Godly) quality of love. In a sense, it is an abuse of the body that God entrusted to the individual's care. To ensure the dignity of marital relations, Jewish law goes to great lengths to see to it that both partners are treated with respect. Some

Chapter Six ————————————————

of these rules are restrictions on when and how marital intimacy may occur.

The reason that the Torah places restrictions on the ways one expresses marital intimacy are out of consideration of Man's lofty stature and his mission in the world; they are certainly not intended to deny pleasure or limit enjoyment. On the contrary, because the Torah places great value on this most precious and beautiful relationship, it guards its sanctity with protective measures that restrict outside forces from defiling its holiness.

As we noted above, the marriage process has two aspects. We translated *nisuin* as related to spiritual uplift. The Hebrew word for the other facet of the marriage process is *kiddushin*, which takes its root and meaning from the Hebrew term *k'dushah*, meaning sanctity. It relates to the idea of separation, of designation of the two individuals as a couple, to the exclusion of anyone else. The groom's public declaration to his bride under the *chuppah, harei at mekudeshet li* ("you are sanctified to me"), creates an intensely personal and spiritual bond between them.

The security, the permanence, the intimacy and warmth of such a marriage creates an environment of holiness and beauty that no substitute can ever provide. This Divinely designed bond is the cornerstone of the Jewish family and continuity; it is largely responsible for

Chapter Six

the unmatched survival of the Jewish people during the most difficult times of persecution, oppression, and exile.

To achieve this invaluable goal, the Torah protects the marriage from outside incursion by requiring both men and women to develop a modest mindset, so that seductive clothing and flirtatious behavior would be curtailed. It also prohibits seclusion with a member of the opposite sex, other than one's spouse, so that infidelity cannot "happen." Think about it. It's a good rule.

Within the marriage, the couple is saved from boredom by the Torah-mandated monthly honeymoon. A period of sexual separation between the couple once a month is followed by a refreshing renewal of their relationship. During the period of separation, the couple must develop self-discipline and non-physical means of communication. This is the vehicle that helps a Jewish marriage outgrow "ice cream love." It creates an environment of mutual respect, appreciation of each other's non-physical qualities, and allows for spiritual growth together. Judaism also has zero tolerance for abuse- physical, verbal, or emotional - and there are Torah laws to back up each spouse's right to dignity and respect. Written thousands of years ago, the Torah legislated human rights laws that are still unheard of in many parts of the world today. Even in enlightened countries, there are dysfunctional marriages in which these basic rules melt under the heat of anger or selfishness, resulting in

Chapter Six ——————————————

bitter lives. If everyone lived by the Torah's rules, family courts would be out of business.

Sounds pretty good, doesn't it? It is. A Jewish marriage that follows the precepts of Jewish law is a harmonious world unto itself. It provides not only the couple with a warm, fulfilling, constantly growing relationship - it also becomes the loving nest in which the next generation is nurtured.

Chapter Six

Intermarriage: A Contradiction in Terms

CHAPTER 7

Intermarriage –
A Contradiction in Terms

We societally often overlook daily absurdities. In a restaurant, we see someone order a piece of rich chocolate cake accompanied by a Diet Coke. We observe another person driving around the health club parking lot for 15 minutes to find the space closest to the entrance. Yet, when people speak of intermarriage, the contradiction does not faze them. Indeed, in Judaism, when a Jew and non-Jew "marry," no legal marriage relationship comes into existence. Intermarriage does not happen.

Why doesn't Jewish law recognize the couple as married? As we noted in the previous chapter, marriage means the unification of the female and male facets of a single soul. These two parts, originally a single unit, were separated and sent to this world to reunite. Souls are categorized in the spiritual dimension according to their missions in this world. Some souls were designed to adhere to the Torah and its commandments - whether because they were present at the Revelation at Sinai, because they subsequently were born to a Jewish mother, or because they converted to Judaism, after its physical birth. This Jewish soul must achieve its own spiritual destiny. Other souls sent down to this life have different spiritual goals and are designed to fulfill the Seven Noahide Commandments.

A young Jewish woman who was dating a non-Jew was upset with this argument. She asked, "Aren't all religions fundamentally the same? They all believe in a Creator and in the same values of honesty, love, and kindness. So what's the difference between them? Since they have essentially the same spiritual outlook, why can't members of different religions marry each other and advance together spiritually?"

Her questions are cogent if we accept her initial premise that "all religions are the same" and that they can have "the same spiritual outlook." Anyone with a deep understanding of any religion will tell you how superficial her argument is. No, they are not the same. They differ in more than just details. A couple disregarding their inherent spiritual incompatibility will not advance together toward their spiritual goals; rather, each will hamper the other.

Chapter Seven ————————————————————

The attempt at marriage between members of the Torah nation - which has one spiritual destiny - and other nationalities, which have totally different spiritual missions - is like trying to merge a philharmonic orchestra with a football team. Neither side will achieve satisfying results for very long. Even if the two can live in the same house and have a physical and emotional connection, their relationship never achieves the purpose of a true marriage. This is why Judaism not only forbids the marriage of a Jew and a non-Jew, it goes so far as to regard both as still single.

The young lady's questions, however, raise other significant points –some by implication - that must be addressed.

Is Opposition to Intermarriage Racist?

If someone is against the marriage of a black woman to a white man, or the marriage of a Norwegian to an Arab, or the marriage of an Ethiopian Jew to an Ashkenazic Jew, that person certainly deserves to be called a racist.

But before we proceed, to be truly honest we must explore the subject of racism itself. When I present the following discussion to Jewish audiences, many present find it disturbing. Yet a sensitive and thinking Jew has no alternative but to come to terms with it.

———————————————— Chapter Seven

Not all that long ago the Jewish people experienced a tragedy of unmatched proportions. Even our nation, with its long history of suffering Inquisitions, Crusades, and pogroms cannot absorb the numbing pain and depth of bereavement that the Nazis and their collaborators heaped upon us. The racist and evil Nazi "ideology" preached the supremacy of the Aryan race. They asserted their right to dominate others whom they deemed inferior- to the point that these "inferior" creatures deserved to be exterminated. Just contemplating this perverse, sick "philosophy" horribly pains us.

But what about us Jews? With all due respect to our cultural accomplishments, are we not infected with the same germ of elitism? Do we not, and others, call us "the Chosen People"? Does not the Torah itself call us "a treasured nation"? Are we ourselves not guilty of the same kind of smugness that ultimately leads to a doctrine of Jewish superiority?

Whenever I pose this question, the comparison between Judaism and Nazism invariably riles members of the audience. They respond, "There is no comparison! The Nazis murdered Jews, Gypsies, crippled children, and homosexuals. The Jewish people's sense of its uniqueness, on the other hand, has never led to the killing or oppression of others."

Chapter Seven ————————————————

"My friends," I answer, "pay attention to what you are saying. You're suggesting that there are two kinds of Nazis. There are Nazi racists like the Germans who are cruel and put their perverse ideology into practice. Then there are the "nicer" Nazis who believe that they belong to a superior race, but do not act on that belief, either because they are cowardly or softhearted. Is this a satisfactory answer to the question that I asked you? Does it ease your conscience?"

So how should we approach this question? Is the concept of a "Chosen People" the same as Aryanism? Is it wrong to make these distinctions between nations?

Our Western culture indoctrinates us from a young age with the idea that any sort of distinction between societies or groups is immoral. We have been taught that making these distinctions always leads to discrimination and oppression. And discrimination against others is abhorrent to us, as it should be. Yet, our zeal to equalize everything sometimes blinds us to the difference between appropriate, justified separation and racist discrimination.

Our sages have taught us that the ability to differentiate between entities is the essence of abstract thought. The scholar's or scientist's main task is to distinguish between closely related concepts or material objects. Without the ability to differentiate, there is nothing to analyze. A fool does not know the difference between day and night, cold and hot, joy and sadness, or wisdom and folly.

We must, however, learn the difference between separation that is just, logical, and natural, and that which is wicked, evil, and contrived. Justified differentiation meets the following two conditions:
- The distinction it makes is based on truth and logic.
- The results of the distinction are relevant to the conclusions drawn from it.

Distinctions based on falsehood - or if they lead to conclusions that are irrelevant to the basis of the distinction - are wrong and evil. Let us go back to my original question comparing Aryanism and Jewish identity.

The Nazis falsely premised their ideology. If we would approach a typical Nazi in downtown Berlin in 1940, we could attempt to check the veracity of his arguments through a simple experiment. The Germans claimed that Aryan blood is superior to that of the rest of mankind. Let's take a blood sample, put it under a microscope, and look for evidence of its superiority.

The test results would immediately contradict his insane claim. But imagine if the argument were found to be correct. Let's say that "Aryan" blood had certain components that made it superior to the blood of others. Does having superior blood (whatever that means) authorize the killing of those who lack it?

On the other hand, let us look at the Jewish people's claim. Is it based on assertions of better blood? No. Our distinction lies in our having committed ourselves to a specific way of life when we accepted the Torah at Mount Sinai. The difference between Jews and non-Jews lies not in our *blood* but in the obligations of our *souls*. Anyone who yearns to do the will of God and live according to the Torah can become a Jew. No one not born an Aryan could ever become one.

So the conclusion that arises from our claim is definitely relevant. Because we accepted upon ourselves a demanding and difficult way of life, we have become a unique nation with a unique mission. We claim no superiority that allows us to do injustice or harm to others. On the contrary, our distinguishing characteristic is that we have accepted upon ourselves the obligation to improve the world by bringing it to the recognition of one God. Therefore, opposition to the marriage of a Jew with a non-Jew has no racial basis but stands on the recognition that we are all the children of God but that each nation has differing specific spiritual needs.

Chapter Seven

"If I'm Not Religious, None of This Really Matters"

You may not buy into the concept above, that the Jewish people have a unique identity and that every Jew has a soul committed to live by Torah law. You might quite naturally reason that if you do not ascribe to the idea of Jewish law and obligation, you can consider yourself absolved from its dictates.

Can you forfeit being a Jew to the extent that its laws no longer apply to you? No. If you were born to a Jewish mother, your spirituality is built into you. You can ignore it. You can choose not to believe it's there. But it won't leave you.

But if you reject Judaism, why should its rules apply? The answer is that you are subject to the laws of Judaism just as you are subject to the laws of any country in which you live, or even visit. The minute you set foot in France, you are subject to French law. As soon as you enter the United States, you must adhere to American law. And the minute you are born a Jew - you began living, as it were, in Jewish land. Unlike other citizenships, it can't be renounced. In Jewish law, you will always be a Jew, no matter what you believe in or what you do.

You may consider this inescapable Jewishness a burden. It is. But it is also a privilege and an opportunity. It leaves the door open for you to explore your connections

Chapter Seven —————————————

with your people and your God at any time in your life. It enables you to take advantage of the Torah's treasures and pass them on to your children.

A marriage that is faulty from the start is one that is based on incompatible spiritual entities trying to forge a new spiritual being. There are those who will argue, "All that you have said is fine and good. But... in my case, I'm *sure* that I've found the one who is meant for me. I simply feel it in my soul. There is no doubt that we were made for each other. It just so happens that she/he isn't Jewish." It is worthwhile to examine the intellectual merits of this claim.

Communion of the Soul vs. Perfect Strangers

Kabbalah is a work of Jewish mysticism. From a kabbalistic point of view, Man's spiritual side comprises three parts: the basic life force (*nefesh*), the spirit (*ruach*), and the soul (*neshamah*). The basic life force, the *nefesh*, is the source of physical life; it is present in animals as well as in Man. The spirit, *ruach*, connects the basic life force with the soul. It includes Man's emotions and his disposition. On the highest level is the soul, the *neshamah*, which is purely spiritual. For a marriage to work, compatibility must exist on all three levels.

We sometimes encounter a married couple who are extraordinarily well suited to each other. They seem so alike, you might think they were brother and sister. Other couples are unusually compatible in a particular area of mutual interest, such as love of nature, music, reading or travel.

Then there is compatibility on a higher level. This includes similar sensitivities and thought patterns. Those who share compatibility of this sort feel that they are really part of a marriage made in heaven.

But this is where the most serious mistake lies. The soul, the most important element of an individual's identity, is higher than the basic life force, and even higher than the spirit. The feelings of the soul leave a very faint impression on our consciousness, for it exists deep within. Because of this, we often confuse the spirit - based on our emotions - with our soul.

When we discussed intermarriage, we made it clear that the problem is neither one of physical nor emotional incompatibility. From a purely physical and emotional point of view, there is a possibility that such a couple will live together harmoniously for a long time, perhaps even for their entire lives. But the soul, the *neshamah*, that must attain perfection, will never attain fulfillment with another soul that does not share its mission. The unity of the *neshamah*'s male and female components will never occur through them. No matter how much they love each other, a Jew and a non-Jew will never be soul mates. Neither has found the intended other half of his or her

Neither has found the intended other half of his or her soul. While he may be a perfectly fine gentleman and she a perfectly wonderful lady as individual human beings, in the context of true marriage they will remain forever-perfect strangers.

So much for the sublime. Let's assume that you accept *none* of the concepts explained until now. The whole idea of the soul and its reunification has no relevance to you; the Jewish "mission" to the world sounds archaic; and the insistence that Jews are bidden to live according to Torah precepts does not impress you.

First of all, if that indeed is the case, I congratulate you for reading this far. It means that, despite your skepticism about the Jewish objection to intermarriage, you have shown enough interest to at least consider the argument.

What you are now hoping to see is less talk of the soul and more discussion of the practical challenges of marrying a non-Jew. You may wonder, apart from all of that spiritual dimension stuff, are there really any good reasons to forgo marriage to the love of your life just because he or she is not Jewish?

Read on.

_____ Chapter Seven

Practical Problems
in Mixed Marriages

CHAPTER 8

Practical Problems in Mixed Marriages

According to the late sociologist and widely renowned intermarriage expert, Dr. Egon Mayer, nowadays over 50% of all marriages end in divorce, whereas the divorce rate of mixed marriages is close to 75%! Most people contemplating intermarriage believe that they of course are the exception to the rule. "We are different," they say, "Our love will last forever!"

As real and serious as the practical problems are, love blurs a clear perspective on them. Yet ignoring or minimizing the difficulties does not make them go away. Let us look at some of them, one by one. There are other, more complex problems that hit some couples, but the ones listed below are the most prevalent and inevitable.

1. Cultural Differences

Our perspective on our experiences in life is built on a network of values whose source lies in our past and in our culture. A person born in India and educated in Buddhist meditation has little in common with an Inuit born near the Arctic Circle engaged in a daily struggle for survival. Although all humanity has a common denominator, culture and values do differ, sometimes drastically.

A Jew's values and culture are deeply rooted in the history of the Jewish people, a complex history cloaked in splendor and replete with suffering. It involves a fine balance between delicate sensitivity and practical common sense, between stubbornness and kindness, between the joy of living and coming to terms with impossible circumstances. Therefore, when a Jew marries a non-Jew, despite all of their hopeful intentions to bridge the gaps and minimize the distinctions, reality will nevertheless surface. When some troubling issue arises, the non-Jew may view it as a simple matter, whereas to the Jew it is something that penetrates the depths of his soul; or the Jew will see it as an open and shut case, while the non-Jew will be filled with doubts.

The Jew is more likely to be aware of anti-Semitism and will be more sensitive to its ramifications. He is likely to need connections with other Jews and with the Land of Israel. He may even find that he is more devoted to some Jewish traditions than he had previously realized. And they will become increasingly important to him as time goes on, particularly when the couple has children. The non-Jewish spouse may well go along with these cultural needs to make things easier, but the Jewish experience and the expressions of Jewishness can never be truly shared. The non-Jew is still an outsider, humoring the Jewish spouse. Likewise, the Jewish partner can empathize, but not fully participate in, his spouse's specific culture.

2. Self-identification

When the mini-series *Roots* was shown on television, thousands, at no small expense, began to examine their genealogical origins. As adopted children mature, they tend to want to know about their biological families. Many people spend much effort and money on assembling a family tree. This is all because, in our hearts, every person is aware that he or she comes from a primeval source and that one's destiny is eternal. We have a need to know from where we come and where we are headed.

Emotionally, many intermarried individuals suffer an identity crisis at some point in the marriage because they know full well that intermarriage constitutes a negation of one's Jewish past. He or she may be aware that the relationship is not even deemed a legal marriage by many Jews. With even the barest Jewish education, most Jews know that over the centuries thousands of Jews chose martyrdom - death - rather than give up Judaism. In Jewish law, the act of intermarrying is considered tantamount to converting to another religion. Despite the best intentions to live a Jewish life, albeit with a non-Jewish spouse, the question of "Am I really a Jew?" perforce gnaws at the individual.

The question is not one of religious identity. It is a matter of coping with the "Who am I?" quandary that every thinking person must eventually face.

3. Holidays

"Okay, this one's a piece of cake," you think. The logic goes: If one holiday is good, two are even better. "Sharing our holidays, doing joint holiday activities, will only enrich our marriage." Because there is no intention of practicing a particular religion exclusively, "We'll have a Chanukah bush and a Christmas tree...On Rosh Hashanah we'll attend synagogue and on Easter we'll go to church."

Sounds like an equal-opportunity household, and that's good, right? The only trouble with the concept is that merging practices, or seesawing from one religion's observances to another, rapidly erodes the meaning of both. At best, they become secular observances with no meaning at all.

Every holiday on the Jewish calendar is actually a celebration of the uniqueness of the Jewish people, to the exclusion of other groups. For example, Passover is a reliving of the Jewish experience of liberation from Egypt through God's mighty hand, with the purpose of galvanizing a nation devoted to His Torah. Its central *mitzvah* (religious obligation) is to tell the story to one's children, to forge the chain of loyalty to the Jewish people, its history, and its goals. One may water down the message of Passover to a general celebration of freedom. But then the richness of the festival, the true meaning of its traditions and its intended purpose, are lost.

In short, by trying to morph the Jewish experience and its holidays into some kind of a uni-religion destroys the essence of Judaism.

4. Children

Anyone who has ever been involved in counseling young people born to intermarried parents is well aware of the depth of the suffering and pain inherent in this sorrowful situation. In my opinion, if a man and woman planning to intermarry have any conscience, they must have their future children in mind. To the couple, no price is too great for the realization of their romantic dream; but, in most cases, their children will pay, suffering with deep emotional problems as a result of their confusion about their "dual identity." As with the erroneous "blending" of the holidays described above, trying to have both yields neither.

I have dealt with couples who felt it was best to give their children educations in both Judaism and Christianity and then give them a choice. The results are generally very poor. The children are simply confused, and they have a distorted view of both religions. You can't get away from the fact that Judaism and Christianity have mutually exclusive ideologies. Christianity preaches that one must believe in Jesus to be "saved." Judaism rejects Jesus entirely. The children, in other words, are given the choice of which part of themselves they will negate. If the children take the decision seriously, they are being set up for massive guilt. Generally speaking, however, both educations are deficient and the children wind up feeling a fidelity to neither. Some will become staunch atheists; other will search for spirituality wherever they think they may find it - in cults, far-Eastern religions, or in pseudo-mysticism.

Another complication arises when the mother of the children is the non-Jew. In Judaism, there are no "half Jewish" children. If the mother is Jewish, the

Chapter Eight ————————————

child is Jewish. If the mother is not Jewish, the child is not Jewish. (Some years ago, the Reform movement embarked on legislating the idea that one can be a Jew based on patrilineal descent - *i.e.*, if the father is a Jew. *No one* - except Reform Jews - accepts this notion. To every other Jew in the world, the child of a non-Jewish mother is not a Jew.) A child given a Jewish education who grows up thinking that he or she is Jewish faces tremendous confusion when that child is ready to marry. If he or she wants to marry a Jew who cares about having a Jewish spouse, major difficulties ensue. (You will find more about this issue in the Appendix , *Children of Inter marriage*.)

"Who says we're planning on having children?" is another reply. Pardon me, but I believe that, generally, a couple starting out their marriage with no intention of having children has a big problem. Somehow, they have failed to develop enough goodness in themselves to see beyond their own selfish needs. They may see children as an encroachment on their freedom; as a financial burden; or as an emotional trap. It will not take long before they view each other in the same light.

Most of the time, couples who say they do not plan to have children are using it as an excuse not to make uncomfortable decisions about the religion of the household. But down the line, they will want children. They will then have to face that their children need spiritual guidance and a heritage that is stable and consistent.

————————————————————— Chapter Eight

5. Family Relationships

Every healthy system of familial relationships requires maximum care regarding the maintenance of harmony, cooperation, and mutual understanding between family members - be they parents, grandparents, aunts, uncles, brothers, sisters, or cousins. When it comes to familial relationships among the intermarried, the challenges and problems are far greater.

A number of years ago a student came to me for guidance with the following story: He was a talented young man who was a member of a successful musical group. The band went on a European tour. He met a young lady from Germany at a concert, they fell in love and before long they were engaged. The wedding was set to take place several months after the engagement.

The young man returned with her to Germany to make arrangements for the wedding and for a place to live afterwards. Of course, he stayed with his fiancée's family, and they had a nice time together.

He was at the peak of happiness and anticipation of the joyous day to come until, a few weeks before the wedding, he had to stay home unexpectedly. His in-laws-to-be didn't realize that he was there and began conversing, thinking he was away. He overheard them talking about the

Jewish son-in-law and his family. Suddenly, he heard such vulgar and venomous anti-Semitic remarks that, on the one hand, he was infuriated and, on the other, frightened. He couldn't believe his ears. Was this a nightmare or the bitter reality? Hadn't they been so welcoming and polite? *Bitte schoen... danke schoen*, and all the rest. How could this be?

He quickly regained his composure, but realized that, like it or not, his wife to be was a part of this family. He packed his bags that night and was on his way to the airport early in the morning. He was completely dumbfounded, but one thing was clear to him - he would never marry someone who was not Jewish.

Does this story represent your average potentially intermarried couple? No. But it certainly reflects a reality, even if not as extreme. Family beliefs and biases are deeply ingrained. To test this, think about how deeply entrenched your family's "truths" are in you, even if you overtly disagree with them.

Family traditions also play a large role in the couple's cultural, recreational, and social lives. The conflicting traditions of the families of intermarried couples are especially manifest at certain times of the year, such as Christmas, Thanksgiving, and Easter. This is true not only for religious Christian families, but for any family that is a product of American culture. Family get-togethers, gift giving, and visiting are all focused around these dates. The typical Jewish family, on the other hand, even if not religious, focuses on the Jewish calendar: Rosh Hashanah, Yom Kippur, Passover, and Chanukah are its important holidays.

In addition, the stories and family anecdotes that are passed on nostalgically from generation to generation, laden with emotion, focus on family experiences. Anybody familiar with Jewish humor and folklore knows how absurd it sounds to someone who has not led a Jewish life and cannot sense the nuances. For the intermarried couple, family get-togethers become a strain. The rich heritages of both sides must be "translated" to the spouse who fails to appreciate it.

6. Family Opposition to the Marriage

I've put this item last because open opposition to intermarriage is declining these days. We must note, however, that the absence of vehement opposition - as was more common a generation ago - does not signify acceptance either. Deep down, the parents on both sides of the intermarrying couple feel they have somehow failed to transmit their family heritage sufficiently. They even may be mystified by their child's choice of a marriage partner. This confusion and disappointment may not manifest themselves openly. The parents may be delighted that "at least" the fiancé is a nice person, well educated, and respectful of their child's background. This is resignation, not enthusiasm.

If the non-Jewish partner is the wife, emotions may flare more when the parents realize that their grandchildren will not be Jewish. Suddenly their Jewishness is important to them. They will pressure the bride to convert, erroneously thinking this will save the situation.

Sometimes emotions go beyond resentment into outright hostility. The couple must contend with a family member who is overtly opposed to their union, will not attend the wedding and will not accept the marriage. Whether or not this attitude is justified is irrelevant: it is the result that concerns us here. For if the person happens to be a parent or grandparent, the couple may suffer considerably from the alienation imposed upon them. Even if they do not mind rejection, their children surely will. They will be deprived of having loving grandparents or great-grandparents in their lives and they will be exposed to the agonies of a family at war with itself.

7. What About These Issues When a Conversion is Involved?

Some of the above mentioned concerns will apply to a proper marriage between a Jew and a properly converted

Jew; those will have to be addressed accordingly. However, in such cases, the lines are clearly drawn and the families and individuals involved have defined parameters which they can work with. Though it does not eliminate the challenges it definitely makes it easier to deal with.

I would like to note that some of the above-mentioned practical dilemmas may be relevant even in cases where an observant Jew marries a non-observant Jew, and once again those are real issues that must be taken into consideration. However, in both situations, i.e., Jew marries convert or Jew marries non-observant partner there are no philosophical/religious problems involved.

Chapter Eight ———————————————

Is Conversion
the Solution?

CHAPTER 9

Is Conversion the Solution?

"If you can't beat 'em, join 'em." But is this the best approach with regard to intermarriage?

At first glance, conversion of the non-Jewish partner to Judaism seems to have its advantages. It will stabilize the home from the standpoint of religion, it will ease tensions with Jewish relatives, and it will moreover convince them of the sincerity of the couple's commitment. When we look into the matter more deeply, however, we find serious problems. For one thing, in sharp contrast to other religions, Judaism does not promote or encourage conversion.

When a non-Jew seeks to convert, one of the main questions that we ask is the individual's motive for conversion. He (or she) might say that he grew up in a Jewish neighborhood and that he loves Jewish culture. He'd die for a pastrami sandwich. Or he feels drawn to the Hebrew language. He is enchanted by the beaches of Eilat and Tel Aviv. He is proud of the way the Israeli army won the Six Day War. Or he really loves…a Jewish girl.

That all sounds very nice, but there is no likelihood that he will be accepted by a Jewish court as a serious candidate for conversion. But why not? He "feels" Jewish, he wants to be a Jew, and he is comfortable sharing his fiancée's heritage. The reason for rejecting him as a potential convert is that, in Judaism, conversion does not mean conversion to a culture, or even to a nationality, in the conventional sense.

Genuine Jewish conversion is permitted for one reason only: sincere and profound recognition of the truth of Judaism, and an intense desire to serve God by committing oneself to the Torah and its commandments, unhesitatingly and forever.

In general, when a mixed couple (married or engaged) wishes to have the non-Jewish partner convert, the sudden interest in conversion has nothing to do with recognition of the Torah's truth. Rather, it has to do with easing the familial and social tensions by unifying the family's identity. Under these circumstances, the motives are *invalid*, and the application for conversion will be rejected.

Even if the non-Jew is sincere in his desire to accept the totality of Judaism, there is an additional problem. Mere intellectual recognition of the Torah's truth is insufficient for conversion. There must also be a conscious, firm commitment to perform *all* of the Torah's commandments, at *all* times, and without exception. We can safely assume that the Jewish partner in a mixed couple is generally not particularly observant. How willing is the Jewish partner to embark on a full Torah lifestyle - including eating only kosher food, maintaining strict Sabbath observance, and dedication to the laws of family purity? How can a potential convert make such a life-altering commitment when his spouse, who was born Jewish, is unwilling to match it?

Keep in mind that once someone has converted with this sincere commitment, even if he later stops being observant, the conversion remains valid - just as someone born Jewish remains a Jew, even if he violates every law of the Torah. Born a Jew or properly converted to Judaism, one remains a Jew, even if not a good one.

A "conversion" that takes place after a few lessons on Judaism, where there is no commitment to live a full Torah lifestyle, is but a formality without substance. Can it be taken seriously by any thinking person? Can it be accepted by Jews who value and protect the sanctity of the Jewish nation? It cannot.

Outside of the Orthodox framework, such "conversions" do take place, and they are counterproductive. The "convert" is led to believe (by clergy with little knowledge, and certainly no expertise in Jewish law) that he or she is fully Jewish, unaware that the conversion is not accepted in Jewish law and is, therefore, worthless. If the "convert" is a woman, she will raise her children to believe that they are Jewish although they are not. The children are the unwitting victims of their parents' ignorance: they are unaware that if their origins are revealed, they will not be accepted universally as Jews. If they marry Jews, they will create more mixed marriages without even realizing it.

The Argument for Damage Control

Experts who worry about Jewish demographics often claim that the only effective response to the growing phenomenon of intermarriage is to convert the non-Jewish partner. They argue that alienating the couple condemns their family to eternal separation from the Jewish nation. From that standpoint, the conversion solution seems both pragmatic and the lesser of two evils. And, indeed, many Jewish organizations and Jewish centers have adopted this approach.

Chapter Nine —————————————————

In addition, there are those who take this concept further and argue that *encouraging* conversion can help the demographic crisis of our dwindling Jewish population (and the resultant dwindling of charitable funds going to Jewish organizations). Note that this approach generally is more concerned with smoothing the statistics and with Jewish PR than helping the couples involved.

Alternatively, organizations have been formed to create a comfort level for couples, with or without Jewish conversion. They jovially promote intermarriage by making it look like fun. I don't know if they truly believe that the serious problems of children in these families can be eradicated by taking them to interfaith workshops to paint Passover plates and Easter baskets. If they do actually think that putting families on this seesaw is beneficial, they are ignoring the essential human need for consistency and stability. They are selling a balm to alleviate superficial discomfort, not a real solution to a deep spiritual problem.

Both concepts - whether it is conversion or comfort- are a disservice to the couple. At their root, they are based on the false premise that intermarriage can work. They lead couples to believe that, indeed, they will escape the 75% probability of divorce. With perhaps the best of intentions, these "solutions" advance what can only be a tragic outcome to the couple and to the Jewish people.

Chapter Nine

It is my hope and prayer that rational, considerate and pragmatic thinking prevail, for the long term benefit of the individuals involved, their families, their children and the future of our nation.

Chapter Nine —————————————————

Appendix 1:
Children of Intermarriage

Appendix I

Children of Intermarriage

Because so many interfaith couples marry, oblivious to the cruelty that they will be inflicting on their future children, I feel it is important to devote more space to this aspect of intermarriage. The following section may draw upon some of the concepts already discussed, but I respectfully ask the reader to consider them in light of the knowledge that you have just acquired by having read until now.

****

Picture this: A person is accused of being a double agent for the United States and for the Soviet Union. The Russians accuse him of having spied for the Americans; the Americans accuse him of having spied for the Russians. He defends himself by saying that his father was Russian and his mother was American, so he loves both countries. He's not to blame for his dual identity. He cares not an iota about any of the political issues. Moreover, he has trouble deciding if he's a Russian with an American mother or an American with a Russian father.

This scenario more or less approximates the feelings of the children of mixed couples. When the child is among Jews, he sometimes feels that they view him as a non-Jew, and when he's in church, people look at him "funny." Even in this society's open and accepting liberal environment, deep inside he feels this conflict.

Many children of intermarried couples "solve" this problem by intellectually siding with only one of the two sides of their dual identity. Some select neither of the two sides, claiming some sort of general universal identity. Despite this, when I speak with many people in this situation, it seems to me that they are continuously grappling with their seemingly dual spiritual/national identity.

It is ironic that often the same people who accuse Judaism of being discriminatory against women do not accept the idea that one is a Jew exclusively through his or her mother's lineage.

Appendix I ———————————————

But it's true that by the Torah law and Jewish tradition of nearly 3,500 years, only the Jewish woman can create Jews. This topic is too large in scope for a full description in these pages, but suffice it to say that it is primarily the mother's duty to conceive her child in purity and in proper manner. Her relations with her husband were preceded by her immersion in a *mikvah* (a small pool of natural water meeting certain religious requirements) in much the same way the Jews immersed in a *mikvah* before entering the Holy Temple in ancient Jerusalem. The marriage is sanctified through her, and the child formed by the couple's union retains that spark of holiness. Yet, even if she didn't fulfill all of these beautiful laws, the mother carries the baby for the next nine months; it is natural that her spiritual identity is transferred to her child. The father's lineage is of lesser relevance from the standpoint of spiritual identity.

Yet if a child of a Jewish mother and a Christian father were to ask a Christian minister what his identity is, he would tell him that he is a Christian with a Jewish mother. And where does that leave the poor child? Totally confused. He may even get the impression that it is up to him to "choose" what identity he accepts.

The same problem confronts somebody with a non-Jewish mother and a Jewish father. In this case, Jewish law determines that the child is not Jewish. Even if after much deliberation and soul-searching, he decides to "identify" as a Jew, the truth is that he does not possess a Jewish soul.

In recent times, new Jewish groups have turned their backs on age-old traditions, many of them proclaiming that a person's identity is entirely his own decision. They assert that someone whose mother is not Jewish is a Jew if he chooses to be. Some have gone so far as to require not even a single Jewish parent: as long as someone "identifies" with Jewish history and experience, he can consider himself a Jew. This runaway situation has caused considerable complications for people who sincerely want to determine who and what they are. The contradictory signals from different "denominations" have resulted in utter confusion. I deal repeatedly with these sad and difficult issues on the college campus.

The upshot of this is that there are many people who are Jews - yet consider themselves non-Jews. Likewise, there are many non-Jews who mistakenly consider themselves Jewish.

Add to this the myth of "half Jew." In Jewish law- as practiced for four millennia from the Revelation at Mount Sinai to this day - there is no such thing as a "half Jew." Either you are a Jew or not. There are no gray areas.

Appendix I ————————————

Incidentally, Judaism does not look down on people who do not have Jewish obligations. Decent people of any background who live by the basic ethical principles common to all mankind (known as the seven Noahide Commandments) can rise to lofty spiritual heights. But they are not Jews. They are not a part of the Jewish people who chose to come nearer to God through fulfilling the Torah's 613 commandments. Should they wish to become a part of the Jewish people, they may join the nation that chose the Torah by also choosing to live by the Torah's laws. They must undergo conversion according to Jewish law, committing themselves to observing the Torah's commandments.

For some children of intermarried parents, dual identity will be a source of ongoing pain. For others, it will signify hypocrisy or disdain for all religions. It should be noted that for some, the road to authentic Judaism will be a long, hard journey, but they will be ready to endure it, even if it entails outright conversion. As the movement toward Jewish religious renewal grows, some children of intermarried couples will find their way to authentic Judaism, likely to the utter dismay of their parents.

Appendix 2:
A Word to Parents and Family

Appendix II

A Word to Parents and Family

Communal Responses to Intermarriage

A town was situated on both banks of a river. A large bridge connected the two parts of the town. After many years of use, the bridge began to crumble and holes appeared in it. The situation deteriorated to the point that one winter, there was a hole so big that a little Fiat fell through it and sank to the bottom of the river with all of its passengers. Of course, ambulances and fire engines sped to the scene of the tragic accident. Through heroic efforts, they managed to haul the car out of the water and save its passengers.

The next day, another small car tried to cross the bridge, and a similar accident occurred. But this time, two passengers died. When the same thing happened on the third day, the town was in an uproar. There were demonstrations in front of city hall complaining about the mayor's negligence. Not only was there loss of life and property, but traffic all over town was tied up because people were trying to avoid the bridge. The economy of the whole region was in danger. The city council convened in an emergency meeting. After three hours of heated discussion, they decided to take drastic measures.

To spare the innocent public further suffering, an emergency first aid station would be built on the riverbank next to the bridge. Traffic on the bridge could thus continue as usual...

This approach is a perfect description of the mindless efforts of many Jewish organizations toward the intermarriage problem. Those who preach "understanding" and "open-mindedness" and recommend coming to terms with the current situation by establishing organizations to help intermarried couples to blend into the Jewish community are systematically building a first aid station next to the rotting bridge instead of fixing the holes.

What is the central problem, the "hole in the bridge" that threatens the Jewish people in our day? It is the Jewish illiteracy and apathy that pervade most of world Jewry. To our great misfortune, this is true even of most Jews who live in Israel.

The historic uniqueness of the Jewish people results exclusively from its devotion to the study of the Torah and the fulfillment of its commandments. When the People of the Book neglect the Book and lose their fervent love of the Torah, the Jewish nation suffers not only spiritual decline, but is threatened with self-annihilation.

The 19th and 20th centuries saw tremendous harm done to the Jewish nation by deviant religious movements that severed the deep bonds that our nation had with its precious heritage - the eternal Torah and its sages, whose teachings attest to their extraordinary genius. Though evil anti-Jewish nations strive to destroy us physically, the ignorance caused by the wholesale defection of Jews to movements that encourage assimilation is annihilating us spiritually. When Jews no longer value their unique obligations and privileges as Jews and feel little connection to God and the Jewish people, intermarriage is the inevitable result.

When I first started dealing with intermarriage issues, I naively contacted a Jewish Community Center and suggested to the administration that they establish an educational program to deal with this painful topic. I was surprised and delighted when they told me that such a program already exists. But then I learned that although there was an educational program on intermarriage, it was *not* aimed at preventing it. On the contrary, its goal was to help intermarried couples fit into the Jewish community.

It was explained to me that some leaders in our Jewish communities view intermarriage as a positive phenomenon. After all, for several decades now, statistics have shown that the world Jewish population is in decline, despite all of the efforts to increase our numbers. The problem is not only for world Jewry at large. It is a problem for the Jewish charitable institutions in particular. A decline in the number of contributors to Jewish charities bodes ill for their continued existence. They therefore see intermarriage as a partial solution to the problem. If intermarried couples can be assimilated into the Jewish community, they and their descendants will identify as Jews and thus increase the number of "Jews" in the world.

This approach constitutes a dreadful error. We must honestly ask ourselves whether concocting artificial solutions constitutes even a reasonable course of action. Will founding a Jewish club, with beautiful swimming pools and gyms for those who still identify themselves as Jews, be able to stop the tragedy of assimilation? Is sending our youth to eat falafel in Eilat and Tel Aviv the wonder drug for which we have been waiting? Bitter reality hits us in the face and shows us that solutions such as these have an effect that at best is meager and temporary. At the very least, they waste precious resources. At worst, they enable the community smugly to feel that it is "doing something" to enhance Jewish identification while in reality it is sending a grotesque mixed message. It is saying "Be

Jewish!" but that Judaism consists of clubs and parties, golf tournaments and an occasional "Mitzvah Day." No wonder thinking Jews find it empty and go elsewhere.

As we look toward the future, there is only one practical solution: we must return to the source, to the study of Torah. Nothing short of a return to a full Jewish life will assure our continued existence. This solution cannot, of course, turn back the clock and wipe away the nightmarish situation in which we currently find ourselves. But it can save what there is left to save.

Will it be easy? No. But any Jew who cares about the future of our people must reach a similar conclusion, even if it painfully contradicts his previous way of thinking. Allow me to use a metaphor that most Jews will recognize: In the years prior to the establishment of the State of Israel, thousands upon thousands of Jews converged on the region, pressed by circumstances to build a new refuge for the Jewish people. Though they were not farmers, they learned how to farm; though they were not builders, they learned to build; and though they were not fighters, they created an army that would fight to the death to protect the Jewish state. To facilitate the ingathering of Jews from countries around the world, the Hebrew language was instituted as the national language and effectively taught to all newcomers. The Hebrew catch phrase for all of these endeavors was *ein brerah*, which means "no choice." There was simply no other way out, no choices to make. It was clear they must survive through these methods or face total destruction.

Today the global Jewish nation faces a challenge at least as formidable. There are Jews who have almost completely blended in with the other nations in a process that has been going on for a number of generations. If they truly want to be part of the glorious future of the eternal nation, they must be encouraged to seek a deep understanding of what that nation is all about. There are many educated Jews who offer to help these seekers find their way to Torah knowledge. These Jews are not missionaries interested in "saving souls." They rather feel a deep concern for their brothers and sisters who have been swept away by the waves of erroneous religious "solutions." They are a resource capable of turning the tide through care and understanding.

The challenge to the Jewish community, therefore, is twofold. On the one hand, the leadership of communal organizations and temples must realize that to save the Jewish nation this is a time of *ein brerah*, no choice. They must increase their allegiance to traditional Jewish observance. Pure, unadulterated Torah will not only help Jews "identify" as Jews, it will nourish their souls and bring new vitality to the community.

The corollary challenge is to the observant community, those Jews whose ancestors struggled faithfully and successfully to hold on to their heritage and who were privileged to raise generations devoted to the Torah. These educated Jews - now large in number - must open their arms and hearts to accept with boundless love the precious Jews looking for help in the study of the Torah and the observance of its commandments. The time for this has never been better, for today more and more thinking Jews are discovering that the Torah is their *only* lifeline.

We see before our eyes a partial realization of the words of the prophet, "Behold, days are coming when I will cast a famine upon the land. Not a famine for bread or a thirst for water. Rather, [a hunger] to hear the words of God" (Amos 8:11). Observant Jews must rise to this challenge and volunteer to educate those who wish to take on a Torah lifestyle, thereby ending the current tragic erosion of the Jewish nation.

Intermarriage and Your Family

It has not been so long since the common practice among Jewish families was to sit *shiva* (the traditional mourning practice for the death of a relative) for a son or daughter who converted out of the faith or intermarried. They would tear their garments in mourning, just as if a close family member had died.

Was their response a display of fanaticism? Was it a demonstration of opposition to anything that did not appeal to their rabbis? No. The mourning was deep and genuine - not for the physical death of a person, but worse, the departure of the soul from living Judaism. To these families, living a life without Torah, without a Jewish attachment to God, was worse than death. To voluntarily cut oneself off from the Jewish people and the basic tenets of Judaism was tantamount to suicide.

This reaction was a true reflection of Jewish values when the most of Jewry was aware of what Judaism means. In our times, however, when the great majority of Jews have been disconnected from authentic Judaism for generations, when people can hardly understand that intermarriage is a problem at all, mourning and sitting shiva is irrelevant. However, cutting off ties with the intermarried couple is also counter productive. In our generation, Jews do not intermarry to rebel against their religious families or to intentionally betray their heritage. They simply have no idea what Judaism is, much the less deliberately abandon it through intermarriage.

I once had a conversation with a young Jew, a friend of one of my students. After about an hour of friendly chat, he mentioned in passing what a sweet girl his fiancée is and the fact that she was quite religious. I turned to him and said, "It seems to me that you've come here with a specific purpose in mind. How can I help you?"

Appendix II ————————————————————————

"You're right, rabbi. I'm here to ask you to do me the honor of officiating at my wedding a few months from now."

This response was completely unexpected, as I did not know this young man well, and I did not know his fiancée at all. But at the same time, I was pleased that he, who did not seem to be observant, was going to marry a religious girl. I imagined that he wanted to become more serious about Judaism and raise a traditional Jewish family. Nevertheless, I was bothered by a question. Why would a religious girl want to marry *him*? Wouldn't the differences in their current lifestyles make their life together impossibly complicated? What would happen on the Sabbath? How could the kitchen be kept kosher?

So I asked him more details about himself and about his family. He seemed to come from a typical Jewish home, non-observant but identifiably Jewish. Then I asked him about his fiancée. What religious school did she attend? Where are her parents from? He answered without batting an eyelash, "She and her family are really very religious. She went to a very strict Catholic school."

I didn't know whether to laugh or cry. Maybe he was playing a practical joke on me? He was serious. He didn't even understand why I was surprised.

He had been educated in the tenets of liberalism in which everyone is the same in all respects. From that point of view, what could possibly be wrong with intermarriage? How could anyone blame him for wanting to marry this girl?

Some families - intentionally or not - punish their child who intermarries in numerous ways. But punishing a young Jew who is unaware of the gravity of intermarriage is like punishing a toddler for getting his shirt dirty with peanut butter. It's irrational. Is the baby at fault?

Defining Intermarriage

Though it may seem a strange thing to do at this juncture, we need to define intermarriage. Allow me to relate another personal incident from my counseling experience.

I once received a phone call from a worried mother. "My daughter," she said slowly, "is dating a non-Jew. Rabbi, I must come talk with you."

She came and we spoke for quite some time. After I listened to her sad story and her tearful request for my help, I asked her a few questions to gain a better picture of the situation. It was obvious that this was a matter of great significance to her. But I had trouble understanding why her daughter's situation should be so painful when the woman herself had jettisoned Jewish tradition. I had a suspicion. So I asked her, "Tell me. Is this non-Jew whom your daughter is dating Caucasian?"

She seemed surprised by the question, but stammered, "What made you think of that?... He's black."

"Interesting," I said. "But if you don't mind, I'd like to ask you another question. Please be perfectly honest with me. If this non-Jewish young man were white, would you be just as troubled?"

This time she smiled wryly and admitted, "I don't think so."

"I'm sorry. I can't assist you in this situation."

She was shocked. "Why not?"

"Your problem," I told her, "has nothing to do with Judaism. It is something altogether different. You simply don't like your daughter's racial choice. For me, race is not an issue. There are black Jews and white Jews and their marriage is perfectly acceptable. Your difficulty is not one for which you turn to a rabbi for help. You should be seeing some other professional to assist you in working through this problem."

As in the story above, quite often parents are upset by their child's marriage choice due to cultural factors, not their loyalty to Judaism. Of course, I was concerned about this impending marriage, but I saw that it was pointless to try to stop it because the mother's attitude was not one of genuine anxiety over interfaith marriage at all. Does the parent's motive matter?

Yes, it matters. Because when a parent objects to a child's intermarriage out of anything less than Jewish conviction, the protest is hollow. The child will know that the objection is due to a bias against the other's religion or nationality – not a serious concern about the child's spiritual welfare. Worse yet, the parents may proclaim that the family will be disgraced in the Jewish community. The child will rightly feel that the parents are more concerned about their social standing than their child's happiness. In these instances, you might as well save your breath.

But if you are truly upset (for meaningful reasons) by your child's plans to intermarry, what should you do? "Sitting *shiva*" may be a proper way to express your agony and dismay, but is ineffective as far as the couple is concerned, and will most likely cause a complete severance of your relationship with your son or daughter. On the other hand, being completely tolerant of the situation simply endorses the union and encourages the marriage to take place.

My experience in this area indicates that the proper approach is a combination of two attitudes that seem to contradict, but actually complement, each other. On the one hand, we show love and understanding to the straying Jew (without condoning his choice). After all, he or she is acting purely out of ignorance of Jewish values. On the other hand, we express absolute rejection of this marriage, which is a detrimental to his/her Jewish soul, a violation of Jewish law and a blow to the Jewish people.

Keep in mind that, as the sages say, "Even if a Jew transgresses the law, he is still a Jew." There is always the possibility that the child will someday awaken to the needs of his Jewish soul and find his way back. This can only be accomplished if his family (and the Jewish community as a whole) takes care not to alienate him and makes it clear to him that he is still beloved.

But - and this is a serious "but" - explain as firmly as possible, in a pleasant manner, that intermarriage is absolutely forbidden for any Jew, and that an intermarriage can never be considered legitimate. For this reason, we cannot take part in the celebration, for it is a sad event that can only cause eventual sorrow for the couple as well as to anyone who holds Judaism sacred. I realize that avoidance of the wedding will likely cause ill feeling, but it is the bottom line.

You may be asked by your child how come you are suddenly so concerned with Jewish law and identity, considering that you have not been a religious Jew in the past. He may even go so far as to remind you that you did not provide a strong Jewish education or role model. Or he may note that you did not seem too concerned over whom he dated in the past, but now that he wants to marry, suddenly you want him to be SuperJew and restrict his marriage choices. What can you answer him? More importantly, what do you tell yourself? Please read the next paragraph very carefully.

Know - with all your heart - that it is not hypocritical to oppose intermarriage, no matter what your personal religious lifestyle has been. For even if you never knew or believed in the tenets of Judaism, never kept a kosher home or fasted on Yom Kippur - the prospect of intermarriage cuts into a Jew's soul. You sense that it is wrong on an entirely different level, a spiritual level that has always been part of you. You know in your heart that you are part of a lineage that goes back to Abraham and Sarah; you know that today you are a Jew because your ancestors resisted every pressure to convert them to other religions; and you know that your child is a link in the eternal Jewish chain, a link you brought into this world. It is perfectly fair and right to expect that child to continue your Jewish heritage with pride.

Speak up with conviction.

No matter what the outcome of your honest, open discussions with your child, you owe it to yourself to view this event as a springboard for your own spiritual growth. Perhaps you never had the chance to investigate authentic Judaism and how it could change your life. This is a good time to find out. There are any number of books, seminars, and online sites that can help you get started. (See the listing at the end of this book.) Just because your child intermarries doesn't make you less of a Jew. In fact, it may open the door to intriguing Jewish studies and deep spiritual fulfillment for you.

If Prevention Was Not Possible

What if the intermarriage has already taken place? In reply to many who have asked me about this topic, I repeatedly stress that it is a disastrous error to accept intermarriage as legitimate after the fact. Although we still value the Jew who has made his mistaken choice and do not blame him, intermarriage itself remains prohibited. In Jewish law the couple is not married. That fact doesn't change, no matter how uncomfortable it may be for everyone.

Practically speaking, we should continue to maintain a relationship with a relative or friend who "marries" a non-Jew. All Jews are responsible for one another, and we must feel sincere and deep love toward each other without exception. The Jewish partner in an intermarriage is a beloved Jew despite everything.

We should relate to the non-Jewish partner politely and considerately. After all, he or she just wishes to spend life peacefully with another person who happens to be a Jew. What could be wrong with that, from their point of view? We must keep in mind when relating to the non-Jewish partner that he or she is a human being created in the image of God, and is someone very special to our Jewish friend or relative.

Relating to the intermarried in a negative or hostile manner is not only unjustifiable, it is counter-productive. It will lead only to a closer relationship between the Jew who is being "persecuted" by his own "fanatic" people and his "enlightened" non-Jewish spouse and family. This will effectively close the door on any possibility of the Jewish spouse eventually reconciling with his or her family and people. Furthermore, if there are children (who are Jewish if their mother is Jewish), having a favorable relationship with the Jewish grandparents and family is more likely to result in the child developing a positive attitude toward Judaism and choosing to marrying Jewish in the future.

Maintaining this delicate balance - clear and uncompromising opposition to the marriage itself, but respect and friendship towards both individuals - is the key to a better future when an intermarriage could not be prevented. While difficult to achieve, it is a most appropriate and effective response to this agonizing and complex situation.

Appendix II ————————

The ideal approach to the perplexing challenge of an interfaith relationship in your family, is to consult with a competent Torah scholar who is familiar with the relevant issues and who is in a position to give proper guidance.

Appendix 3:
The Eternal Jewish Family Solution

Appendix III

The Eternal Jewish Family Solution

For couples of interfaith marriages who are sincerely looking to rectify their unfortunate fate and provide an honest resolution for their children's future, there is not only hope, but a real and doable solution. It is called The Eternal Jewish Family. This newly formed organization aims to help such couples with a procedure of proper preparation for a universally accepted halachic conversion. It provides adequate Jewish education for the family coupled with Rabbinical and social counseling to guide them through the sometimes challenging process. Though this effort is relatively new, it has already produced impressive results, helping many such family units attain a practical, permanent and halachicly correct closure to a painful dilemma.

For more information and contacts, see Appendix IV.

139

Appendix 4: Recommended Reading

Appendix IV

Recommended Reading

Outlook and Philosophy

HANDBOOK OF JEWISH THOUGHT – Rabbi Aryeh Kaplan (Moznaim 1979)
A veritable encyclopedia of Jewish philosophy. A highly systematic and exhaustively-researched treatment of virtually every theological issue including God, prophecy, the Messiah, reward and punishment, the Sinai experience and the Oral Law. Fully referenced and sourced. Essential reading.

THE WAY OF GOD – Rabbi Moshe Chaim Luzzatto (Feldheim 1988)
This 18th century classic is a standard text in every yeshiva throughout the world. A thorough, intellectual

examination of the whys-and-hows of the relationship between God and mankind, Jews and non-Jews, and the physical and metaphysical worlds.

ON JUDAISM – Emanuel Feldman (Shaar Press 1994)
In the form of conversations between a rabbi and a seeker, this book delightfully weaves through the fabric of Jewish life including faith, covenant, ethics, sin, holiness, prayer and more. The author, besides being a law school professor and magazine editor, is the rabbi who built Torah Judaism in Atlanta from the ground up.

IF YOU WERE GOD – Rabbi Aryeh Kaplan (NCSY 1983)
Three masterful essays: understanding God by putting oneself in His role; immortality and the soul; and the purpose of creation.

PERMISSION TO BELIEVE/ PERMISSION TO RECEIVE – Lawrence Keleman (Feldheim 1990, 1996)
Two articulate and cogent presentations of the assertion that (despite conventional attitude to the contrary) an intelligent, critical, and rational person may, or even should, accept the veracity of Torah Judaism. Straight intellectual approach. Includes an outstanding section on Torah and Science. Highly recommended.

STRIVE FOR TRUTH – Rabbi Eliyahu Dessler (Feldheim 1985)
Very accessible exploration of deep Jewish concepts like

Reward and Punishment, Emulating God, and Love. Based on Rabbi Dessler's classic Hebrew work, "Michtav M'Eliyahu."

LET US MAKE MAN – Rabbi Abraham Twerski (CIS 1989)
This world –renowned psychiatrist presents the Jewish view on mental health. A plan for discovering true self-awareness. Includes: humility, dignity, self-esteem and peace of mind.

THIS IS MY GOD – Herman Wouk (Doubleday 1959)
This famous contemporary author explains why he prays, studies Talmud daily, and walks with a constant awareness of being Jewish. Beautiful, poetic and inspiring.

FUNDAMENTALS AND FAITH – Rabbi Yaakov Weinberg (Targum 1991)
The dean of Ner Yisrael, one of the largest yeshivas in America, explains Maimonides' "13 Principles of Faith." Includes: God, Prophecy, Revelation, and the Messiah.

THE INFORMED SOUL – Rabbi Dr. Dovid Gottlieb (Arrtscroll-Mesorah 1990)
Essays from a former Professor of Philosophy at Johns Hopkins University now turned Rabbi. Includes: comparative religion, Chosen People, suffering, mysticism and Teshuva.

FINGERPRINTS ON THE UNIVERSE – Louis Pollack (Shaar Press 1994)
Searching for belief and meaning in today's turbulent world. Includes issues of science, enlightenment, and modern psychology.

NINETEEN LETTERS – Rabbi Samson Rafael Hirsch (Feldheim)
Formatted as a series of letters answering a student's inquiries on Torah, this work boldly answers the charge that Torah Judaism is old, decadent and irrelevant.

CHOOSE LIFE – Rabbi Ezriel Tauber (Shalheves 1991)
This Holocaust survivor grapples with the questions: Do I believe life is precious? What does God want from me? Is true happiness attainable? How do I turn the mundane into the meaningful?

Rabbi Zelig Pliskin's Self-Help and Growth

GATEWAYS TO HAPPINESS
Your attitude controls your mood. Learn the Torah's techniques for ridding yourself of anxiety, fear and stress – while increasing your joy, appreciation and energy.

GUARD YOUR TONGUE
Gossip is one of the most negative and destructive activities humans can do. The Torah provides clear, practical guidelines for avoiding this trap. Adapted from the classic work, "Chofetz Chaim."

BEGIN AGAIN NOW!
A concise encyclopedia of strategies for healthier living – from A-to-Z. Features practical techniques on: Celebration, Confidence, Accomplishment, Reframing and Visualization.

Jewish Law and Observance

TO BE A JEW – Rabbi Hayim Halevy Donin (Basic Books 1972)
A complete guide to Jewish observance in contemporary life. Clearly explains the origin and practice of every holiday and ritual. Great refresher course or re-introduction to our rich heritage.

TO PRAY AS A JEW – Rabbi Hayim Halevy Donin (Basic Books 1980)
A systematic exploration of prayer and the synagogue, which both the beginner and expert will find extremely informative and useful. Analysis of the Amidah, Shema, Kaddish and grace after meals.

HOREV – Rabbi Samson Rafael Hirsch (Soncino 1962)
Review of the details and reasons for mitzvahs, in light of the struggles of modern man.

GATEWAY TO JUDAISM – Rabbi Mordechai Becher (Shaar Press, 2004)
The what, how and why of Jewish life.

Shabbat and Holidays

THE BOOK OF OUR HERITAGE – Rabbi Eliyahu Kitov
(Feldheim 1978)
A thorough review of the Jewish calendar. Includes
month-by-month explanation of all the holidays, laws and
customs throughout the Jewish year. A classic.

FRIDAY NIGHT AND BEYOND – Lori Palatnik (Jason
Aronson 1994)
The "How-To" book on the authentic Shabbat experience.
Filled with step-by-step instructions, answers to common
questions, and warm personal anecdotes. Highly
recommended.

ROSH HASHANA AND YOM KIPPUR SURVIVAL
KIT – Shimon Apisdorf (Leviathan Press 1994)
The award-winning guide to getting more meaning out of
the High Holidays. With humor and sophistication, this
book offers invaluable insight to the significance of the
holidays and prayers. User-friendly format.

SURVIVAL KIT HAGGADAH – Shimon Apisdorf
(Leviathan Press 1994)
This Passover, don't just eat the Matzoh and bitter herbs—
find out "why!" Explanations of all the symbolism and
historical background of the Seder rituals.

Marriage and Family

MARRIAGE – Rabbi Zelig Pliskin
A comprehensive guide to enhancing any marriage. Basic Torah concepts including practical insights from a master counselor. Scores of fascinating illustrative stories.

MADE IN HEAVEN – Rabbi Aryeh Kaplan (Maznaim 1983)
The complete guide to how to make a Jewish wedding. A compendium of customs and traditions, along with mystical and historical explanations. Includes discussions of the Chuppah, the ring, the Ketubah and more. Don't get married without it!

THE RIVER, THE KETTLE, AND THE BIRD – Rabbi Aharon Feldman (Feldheim 1987)
Culled from 3,000 years of wisdom on how to have a successful marriage, this best-selling book is the authoritative guide to "Shalom Bayis" (peace in the home). Examines topics like anger, listening, respect, dignity, men and women, and sex.

TO BECOME ONE – Rabbi Ezriel Tauber (Shalheves 1990)
A deep look at the dynamics between Adam and Eve, and the differences between men and women that we see in our own time.

JEWISH ALTERNATIVES IN LOVE, DATING AND MARRIAGE – Rabbi Pinchas Stolper (NCSY 1984)
A secure and sensible perspective on the challenges of love, dating and marriage. Aimed at the young reader, from a traditional perspective.

HEAD TO HEART – Gila Manolson (Targum 2005)
What to know before dating and marriage.

The Jewish Woman

TO BE A JEWISH WOMAN – Dr. Lisa Aiken (Jason Aronson 1992)
The long-awaited compendium of issues for the modern Jewish woman. Includes issues of the synagogue, child raising, modesty, the Mikveh, and spirituality. Plus a historical overview of the Matriarchs.

OUTSIDE INSIDE – Gila Manolson (Targum 2002)
Modesty and the inner dynamic of women and men.

THE MAGIC TOUCH – Gila Manolson (Feldheim 1992)
A Jewish approach to relationships.

OUR BODIES OUR SOULS – Tzipporah Heller (Targum 2003)

Parenting

POSITIVE PARENTING – Rabbi Dr. Abraham J. Twerski, M.D. and Ursula Schwartz, Ph.D.
Instead of asking "where have we gone wrong?" this book helps us to concentrate on how to do things right, and especially how the Torah and Jewish tradition counsel us to chart our children's paths. Filled with practical wisdom and advice, this book should be reviewed and pondered over and over again. A treasure.

MY CHILD, MY DISCIPLE – Rabbi Noach Orlowek (Feldheim 1993)
International lecturer and counselor to thousands. Rabbi Orlowek demonstrates how to implant discipline in your children and how to close the generation gap. Clear and concise. A must.

MAKE ME DON'T BREAK ME – Rabbi Moshe Gans (ArtScroll-Mesorah 1994)
How to motivate children for success at home and in the classroom. Full of real-life situations which apply Torah techniques to help maximize the potential of children and students.

The Aryeh Kaplan Series

Rabbi Aryeh Kaplan emerged in the 1970s as the most articulate voice of today's generation. Listed in "Who's Who" as an accomplished physicist, Aryeh Kaplan applied his brilliant mind first and foremost to Torah study – mastering all the works of Jewish philosophy, law and Kabbalah. He shared his encyclopedic knowledge in a series of masterful works that blends the mystical and the practical. His death at the age of 48 left a void which remains until today.

SABBATH: DAY OF ETERNITY*
How Shabbat is a taste of the Messianic Age and the World to Come. (NCSY)

TEFILLIN: God, Man, Teffilin*
Practical and philosophical exploration of Man's search to unite with God. (NCSY)

TZITZITH; A THREAD OF LIGHT*
How these threads are the essence of passion, free will, and self-control (NCSY)

WATERS OF EDEN*
The mystery of the Mikvah. (NCSY)

JERUSALEM : EYE OF THE UNIVERSE*
Reveals the depth of Judaism's holiest site. (NCSY)

Appendix IV ————————————————

THE REAL MESSIAH*
A Jewish response to missionaries. (NCSY)

THE INFINITE LIGHT: A BOOK ABOUT GOD*
What the Kabbalists say about the highest spiritual dimensions. (NCSY)

IF YOU WERE GOD*
Three essential essays on God, the soul and afterlife. (NCSY)

MAIMONIDES PRINCIPLES*
Exploration of the 13 Fundamentals of Jewish Faith. (NCSY)

JEWISH MEDITATION
Mantras, unification, and conversing with God. (Schocken)

THE HANDBOOK OF JEWISH THOUGHT, Vol. I, II
Jewish philosophical concepts from A-to-Z. (Maznaim)

THE LIVING TORAH
Modern, fresh translation of the Five Books of Moses. (Maznaim)

NOTE: Books with an asterisk (*) are available in a two-volume compilation entitled "The Aryeh Kaplan Anthology." (NCSY-Mesorah)

Teshuva – Return to Judaism

ANATOMY OF A SEARCH – Dr. Akiva Tatz (ArtScroll-Mesorah 1987)
A young, affluent South African surgeon traces his disaffection with Western secular society, and contrasts it with the advantages he found in the Orthodox way of life.

THE BAMBOO CRADLE – Avraham Schwartzbaum (Feldheim 1988)
While on Sabbatical in Taiwan, an American professor and his wife find a newborn baby girl abandoned in a railroad station. When they adopt and raise the Chinese infant, their desire to provide her with a Jewish education eventually leads them to a Torah lifestyle. An excellent account of the intellectual and social processes experienced along "the road back." Heartwarming, amusing and educational.

THE ROAD BACK – Rabbi Mayer Schiller (Feldheim 1978)
In search for his spiritual roots and identity, the author sets out on a rigorous educational program. Includes an examination of assimilationist movements in light of traditional Judaism, and a stunning contrast of Western versus Jewish thought.

FROM CENTRAL PARK TO SINAI - Roy S. Neuberger (Jonathan David Pub. 2002)
A fascinating story of an exceptional family's journey from secularism to Jewish observance.

The Holocaust and anti-Semitism

A PATH THROUGH THE ASHES
SPARKS OF GLORY
THE UNCONQUERABLE SPIRIT (ArtScroll-Mesorah)
This series features inspiring vignettes of spiritual fortitude in the face of the Nazi terror.

Jewish Contribution to Civilization

WORLDPERFECT – Rabbi Ken Spiro (Simcha Press, 2002)

Jewish History

TRIUMPH OF SURVIVAL – Berel Wein (Shaar Press 1990)
The complete story of the Jews in the modern era, 1650-1990. Filled with facts and anecdotes. Includes: Enlightenment, anti-Semitism, American Jewry, the Holocaust, and the State of Israel. Drawn from Rabbi Wein's masterful cassette lecture series.

HERALD OF DESTINY – Berel Wein (Shaar Press 1990)
The complete story of the Jews in the medieval period, 750-1650. Far from the "Dark Ages," this is a time when Jews achieved great heights of power, wealth, scholarship and creativity. Includes: Maimonides, the Golden Age of Spain and the Spanish Inquisition, and the rise of Kabbalah. Entertaining, informative, inspiring.

ECHOES OF GLORY – Berel Wein (Shaar Press)
The story of the Jews in the Classic Era – 350 BCE-750 CE. From the Second Temple Era to the times of the Geonim. It includes: the compilation of the Mishnah and Talmud, and how they saved Jewish life for all time; such great Geonim as Rabbi Saadia, Rabbi Sherira, and Rabbi Hai, and how they led the monumental Torah centers of Babylonia and North Africa; the rise of Christianity and Islam and the Jewish response; Jewish life taking root in the barbarous lands of Europe.

FATE AND FAITH: THE STORY OF THE JEWS IN THE TWENTIETH CENTURY – Berel Wein (Shaar Press 2004)
This history explains the foundations of today's American Jewish mentality.

Appendix IV ————————————————

Pluralism

JEWS FOR NOTHING – Rabbi Dov Aharoni-Fisch
(Feldheim 1984)
An analysis of why Jews fall victim in such large numbers
to intermarriage, assimilation and cults.

WHO IS A JEW? – Rabbi Jacob Immanuel Schochet
(Shofar 1987)
A calm, rational and sensitive explanation of why
Orthodox Judaism does not accept Reform or Conservative
conversions.

Intermarriage

WHY MARRY JEWISH? – Doron Kornbluth
Surprising reasons for Jews to marry Jews.

Non-Jews

THE PATH OF THE RIGHTEOUS GENTILE – Rabbi
Chaim Chlorfene and Yakov Rogalsky (Targum 1987)
An overview of the spiritual path reserved for non-Jews,
with a delineation of the Seven Laws of Noah.

Torah and Science: Religious Perspective

The ranks of Orthodox Jewry include many outstanding scientists who have successfully grappled with the apparent conflicts between Torah and science. The volumes and journals listed here treat one or more of the major issues, including Evolution, the Big Bang, and the Age of the Universe.

GENESIS AND THE BIG BANG – Dr. Gerald Schroeder (Bantam 1990)
A groundbreaking work that confronts the cosmological debate head-on. The author, a former M.I.T. professor of nuclear physics and member of the U.S. Atomic Energy Commission, is now a Discovery lecturer in Jerusalem

CHALLENGE – Rabbi Aryeh Carmell and Cyril Domb (Feldheim 1978)
Thirty-four articles presenting the Torah View on Science and its Problems. Includes: nuclear physics, biology, environmentalism, genetic engineering, and extra-terrestrial life.

Jewish Outreach Organizations

College Outreach

ELIYAHOO
www.eliyahoonetwork.com
info@eliyahoonetwork.com

JAAM
www.jaam.net
rabbif@umich.edu
734-996-2000

SINAI RETREATS
www.sinairetreats.com
info@sinairetreats.com
301-807-2434

For Intermarried Couples

ETERNAL JEWISH FAMILY
www.eternaljewishfamily.org
info@horizons.edu
845-425-3863

General Outreach

ARACHIM
www.arachimusa.com
East Coast: 718-633-1408
West Coast: 818-343-9347

AISH HATORAH
www.aish.com
tellus@aish.com
972-2-628-5666

HINENI
www.hineni.org
hineni@hineni.org
212-496-1908

GATEWAYS
www.gatewaysonline.com
office@gatewaysonline.com
1-800-722-3191

OHR SOMEACH
www.ohr.edu

Dedicated in loving
memory of our dear
Bubby and Zada
**Pauline and Louis
Hammerstein**

*Mr. & Mrs. Brent Triest
Mr. & Mrs. Glenn Triest*

Dedicated in honor of

Rabbi & Mrs. Avraham Jacobovitz

Drs. T. Barry & Arlene Levine

Dedicated in honor of our children and Grandchildren

Nina & Howard Greenstein
Desbe, Maya, Samuel

Amy & Dov Carl
Samantha, Matthew, Hannah, Daniel

Sherri & Rabbi Raffie Zuroff
Yakira, Mordechai, Zahava, Noam

Mr. & Mrs. Seymour Greenstein

Dedicated in loving
memory of

Bert Loebmann

*The Loebmann Family
Chicago, IL*

Dedicated in loving
memory of

Dr. Milton Shiffman

*Lois Shiffman
& The Shiffman Family*

Dedicated in loving
memory of

Mr. M. Leo Storch

Dedicated in loving
memory of

Mrs. Esther Stein
אסתר בת חנניה
January 1, 2006
י"ב טבת תשס"ו

Mr. Phillip Stein
פנחס בן שלמה זלמן
December 26, 1997
כ"ז כסלו תשנ"ח

רפואה שלמה לאבי מורי יעקב בן אלישבע

משפחת טוויל

Dedicated in loving
memory of
פעריל בת מרדכי

In Honor of
אהרן בן יעקב
מנחם בן נתן
ליבי רחל בת מיכאל

And in appreciation of
Rabbi Avraham and Bayla
Jacobovitz